Growing Strong Girls

Growing

PRACTICAL TOOLS TO CULTIVATE CONNECTION

Strong

IN THE PRETEEN YEARS

Girls

LINDSAY SEALEY, MA ED

FOUNDER OF BOLD NEW GIRLS

A LifeTree Media Book

CATALOGUING DATA AVAILABLE FROM LIBRARY AND ARCHIVES CANADA

ISBN 978-1-928055-29-7
ebook ISBN 978-1-928055-30-3

Published by LifeTree Media Ltd.
www.LifeTreeMedia.com

Distributed by Greystone Books Ltd.
www.greystonebooks.com

LEAD EDITOR Michelle MacAleese
EDITOR Judy Phillips
DESIGNER Setareh Ashrafologhalai
AUTHOR PHOTO Lindsay Faber
Printed and bound in Canada
Distributed in the United States by Publishers Group West
17 18 19 20 21 5 4 3 2 1

To all of you who nurture, support, and champion girls to be strong and confident from the inside out—intentionally growing strong girls and cultivating connection is the most important and profound privilege we share.

Contents

Foreword

IF YOU ARE a parent or another "big person" invested in raising and championing a girl, you are holding the most wonderful gift in your hands in the form of this book. Having worked with children and families for many years, there is one thing I know for sure: connection is at the heart of what makes the world go 'round.

The science of child development has irrefutably revealed that the most central need all children everywhere have for healthy development is relational connection. When a child is held in the space of nurturing connection by their special adults in all aspects of their life—home, school, sport, community—something incredible happens in the core of their emotional brain. Neural track gets laid down that promotes regulation, reduces stress, increases resiliency, and fosters optimal outcomes academically, socially, and eventually, professionally.

Sadly, today's girl is growing up at a time when much of what would once have "just happened" naturally to support her healthy development now has to be carefully mapped out. The cultural norms and social structures of generations past that would have ensured a girl grew up in a general milieu of relational connection have been squashed by the intensity of our fast-paced modern lives. And unfortunately, this erosion of culture and context for her healthy development has also happened at a time when she is most vulnerable. Never before have the pressures and stresses of life been so marked for the growing girl; they bear down upon her in her young years and chase after her as she heads into the class-room and the community. She must be ready to learn, ready to excel, ready to conquer in our current culture of success-seeking social pressures.

What Lindsay Sealey offers in this accessible, applicable, and informed read is brilliant insight into the psyche of the growing girl. This insight forms the foundation of a call to action for parents, teachers, and other adults that Sealey most capably maps out. I have had the privilege of seeing Lindsay Sealey connect to countless parents and teachers, encouraging them to nurture the girls they are growing up. Her remarkable capacity to see through the noise of life and right into the hearts of the girls she supports in her work is what makes her the rarest and most brilliant gem. And it is exactly that wisdom that permeates every page of this book.

So often as adults we want strategies and tools and solutions. We want a magic list of steps to "fix" a perceived problem or side-step our worries. But never has such a list been proffered that actually *works*. The problem with coming at things with precon-ceived lists is that they fail to honour the deeply seated emotional intricacies unique to each person. Lindsay Sealey knows this and has deftly avoided such a trap. Instead, she reveals the profoundly important need that all girls have to connect with their own self. It is only when a girl can find silence in the midst of the world's chaos that she can truly see herself as a whole, soulful, and wor-thy being. From a place of understanding who she is, a girl can then confidently walk forward in sharing her light with the world around her. It is when we have connected to ourselves in caring and compassionate ways that we can then connect with others empathically and supportively.

As an adult, when you give a girl your time, your interest, your enthusiasm, your confidence, you create an environment for inner growth that will most certainly propel her forward in a way that she can then meaningfully connect with and contribute to her world. And from there, anything is possible. Change-maker, innovation seeker, compassion warrior. Whatever your girl sets her sights on will be possible when she has the most cherished experience of growing up in connection with you, connection with others, and eventually, connection with the world.

Growing Strong Girls provides the foundation for understanding why connection is so important—from the inside out. You can transform this understanding into action. Perhaps you only need some affirmation that you are on the right track, or maybe you are feeling absolutely bereft at having "lost" your girl to the pressures of the world. Either way, you have landed precisely where you needed to because you are reading this book.

As Lindsay Sealey will show you, there is always hope. Your girl needs you and all you need to do to be the answer for her as she charts her course forward is to be present. In your presence, you create a space for her to grow. There is an intangible invitation for her to exist. There is emotional safety and rest that releases her to find courage. And when a girl can connect with that, there is no telling what she will be capable of. If all the adults everywhere could live and breathe the wisdom contained in *Growing Strong Girls*, we could change the world . . . one strong girl at a time!

Dr. Vanessa Lapointe, R. Psych
Founder of the Wishing Star Lapointe Developmental
Clinic and author of *Discipline Without Damage: How
to Get Your Kids to Behave Without Messing Them Up*
Vancouver, 2017

Introduction

GROWING STRONG GIRLS. What, you may be thinking, is a "strong girl," exactly, and how on earth does one grow one? Let me explain. Strong girls are those who use healthy ways to connect to their deeper self, and to the world around them. Strong girls listen to their inner voice and follow their intuition. They have a clear sense of self: they know who they are and what they need. Strong girls view mistakes as opportunities to learn and grow. They think for themselves, ask for what they need, set boundaries, and can stand up for themselves. Strong girls know they matter and have self-respect. They have the courage to stand strong in their truth and own their unique stories. They believe in themselves enough to step out of their comfort *Strong girls know they matter* zones and take positive risks to live authentic and happy lives. This world needs strong girls—girls who are calm and authentic, who are bold and unapologetic, and who are true to themselves.

Yet growing up is challenging. All of you who were little girls or who love one will know what an understatement that is. And all too often, somewhere between ages nine and fourteen, girls who were born bold—centred and funny and uninhibited—lose their sparkle. A growing girl has so many changes to deal with all at once: a changing body, a changing brain, fluctuating emotions, and shifting friendships, among other life changes. As adults, we know well that life doesn't let up and that our best defence is to cultivate inner strength so we can navigate all life's challenges as they come. In the unpredictable, tumultuous time of these preteen years, girls need security; that is where constancy in relationships with family members, teachers, counsellors, and mentors becomes critical. In other words, if they are to be strong girls, they need us! They will do amazing things if given the conditions to thrive, and we, as caring parents, mentors, and teachers, can work to remove the barriers that get in their way. I know how challenging it is to watch girls grow up, and have felt that instinct to protect them from making mistakes and having to learn about life the hard way.

They will do amazing things if given the conditions to thrive

So, how do we grow strong girls? By cultivating connection. At the heart of everything I explore in this book is the value of connection: consistent, unconditional nurture, care, concern, and comfort. Connection is the feeling of being seen, heard, valued, and validated without judgment or conditions, leading to fulfillment and a deep sense of belonging and inclusiveness. Connection is the opposite of isolation, separation, and desolation. It is the sharing of experiences, whether successes and joys, or losses and pain. Such connection will keep girls on the path to strength, well-being, and success. When girls feel connected and safe, they can walk through life with a sense of certainty, security, and power.

After fifteen years and working with hundreds of girls, I've seen it all. Some girls find school and learning easy; others struggle to keep up. Some girls are social; others are shy. Some girls are athletic; others are artistic. Although a few girls are confident, most girls only *seem* confident while actually struggling with knowing who they are and with sharing their true voice and opinion. But one thing they all have in common is a desire to connect. I have yet to meet a girl who doesn't want to fit in and feel a sense of belonging and closeness. Yet, despite this yearning to connect, many don't have the words, tools, or maturity to make it happen.

Girls want to know that you "get" them, but this is hard when they don't always have the communication skills to articulate the realities of their world or the pressures they feel. One thing all the girls I've worked with have been clear about is that they feel misunderstood—"My parents just don't understand." Meanwhile, parents tell me they wish for a stronger connection with their daughters and tell me, "I can't get through to her." There is a way to understand each other again. My intention in this book is to bridge the gap, to be the interpreter between girls and those who seek to support and champion them, which I've been doing in my work as an educator and coach with hundreds of families. I've seen it time and again: instead of using the go-to tools of criticizing, blaming, and entering into power struggles, parents learn to listen better, empathize more, and think before responding. With sincere intention and repeated practice, making connection a habit, families do reconnect, and girls can get back on track.

There is a way to understand each other again

Today's world teaches a girl—explicitly and implicitly—to disconnect from herself and to seek happiness and fulfillment outside herself. Through media messages and their emphasis on beauty, sex, and perfectionism, girls are being told they are not good enough. And they are living in a world of cyberbullying, microcelebrity (creating their own "brand" and the inner experience of being "famous"), hypersexualization, and social media addiction. It's no wonder their mental health concerns are on the rise and their fragile self-esteem is plummeting. Because the reality is this: girls are feeling less happy, less connected, and less fulfilled than ever.

Even given all these social trials and tribulations, the greatest source of disconnection for a girl is her unhappiness with herself. We are our own worst critic. A girl disconnects from her true self whenever she conforms to the wishes of her peers, when she tries to be someone she is not. Feeling disconnected is detrimental to a growing girl—she becomes susceptible to feeling isolated, different, lost and lonely, even depressed. In extreme cases, it can lead to self-rejection and self-harm. As a model for how she can connect to her true self, give her the example of connection with you.

Neuroscience supports that we are hardwired for connection. Secure attachment is the basis for healthy self-esteem, healthy cognitive and social development, impulse control, and general success in school. We have a need for emotional contact and

They need you

responsiveness from the significant people in our lives, and that need never disappears.[1] This is not a hope; this is biology. The more we connect, the safer and more secure we feel, which contributes to our emotional, physical, mental, social, psychological, and spiritual health. The groundbreaking work on attachment by Mary Ainsworth and John Bowlby has helped us see that attachment is an integral part of human behaviour throughout the whole lifespan, and the more dependent people are on one another, the more independent and daring they become.[2]

When children feel a secure connection to and dependence on you, they feel a sense of harmony, belonging, and reciprocal bonding. They get a strong sense that they matter. This need for secure attachment never goes away, even in adults.[3] Secure connection is tremendously valuable in increasing confidence and positive moods, as well as decreasing stress, anxiety, and mental health challenges. It is exactly what promotes healthy development and makes growing strong girls possible.

How to Connect

So, I think we can all agree on the importance of growing strong girls. And we now know that cultivating connection is the key. But how exactly do we do *that*?

As a parent, you may be wondering, "How do I help my daughter connect with herself when she is constantly critiquing and putting herself down, when she is so hard on herself?"

As a teacher you may be wondering, "How do I help the girls in the classroom connect with each other when they are so competitive, when they seem to share so little in common, or when some seem so much more mature than others?"

As a counsellor, mentor, or coach, you may be wondering, "How do I help her see that she is so much more than how her body looks, and that she really can make a difference in the world?"

When she connects with you, she can relax and come to understand that she can also trust herself and her inner voice of guidance. It's a vibrant connection with you that creates the conditions necessary for her to develop and maintain a connection with her true self and with others in the world.

Girls need your time

In a recent workshop I facilitated with a group of grade-five girls, I handed each girl a blank card and asked her to write down her answer to this question: What do you most need from your parents or an adult in your life? Without hesitation, the girls wrote down their answers. Later, I read the cards. Every single one expressed the identical need: time with you. In other words, they need *you*. We need to make and take more time for them.

Girls need your time. This is key. They need time to unburden themselves of their worries and fears. They need time to talk out what is happening in their inner world, to figure out who they are. They need time to ask questions when their lives feel confusing or complicated. When a girl trusts you will be there for her, she navigates the world from a place of security and inner strength. She comes to know that no matter how bad her day is, she can come to you to safely express a rainbow of feelings and be heard. All she has to do is explore and express her inner world, and trust that her needs will be met with your loving kindness, acceptance, and empathy. She'll feel your presence and she'll feel connected.

You may have doubts at times. I have doubts too. You may wonder, "Am I making a difference? Am I doing this right?" You may feel that your words are falling on deaf ears or that the lessons you are imparting are not being heard. You may have also experienced the "push and pull effect," where she both pushes you away to create her sense of autonomy and pulls you in to feel a sense of connection with you. I have to confess, there are days when I give advice more than I listen, because I am so eager to "fix" her problem with a three-step plan of action. I fully understand the delicate balance of wanting to "lock down" to keep her close to you and "letting go" to release her to grow in her independence. On those days when you are not sure you are making a difference, when you're struggling to find that balance, or you wonder if you're doing too much talking and not enough listening, remember this simple truth: If you're there, you're doing it right.

How This Book Is Structured

This book is for parents, teachers, counsellors, mentors, coaches, older siblings, caregivers, and companions... anyone who is a champion for girls and is willing to give them their time. Each of the three parts of this book explores an aspect of the kind of connection a girl needs and the ways in which we can help her cultivate that connection.

Part 1 charts a girl's journey inward. It looks at how you can help a girl cultivate a connection with her true self by leading her to explore, love, and accept her whole self, and to be appreciative of what is happening inside by paying mindful attention to her body and staying grounded in her lived experience.

Part 2 follows a girl's journey outward as she connects in relationship with others. This section covers how to avoid social comparisons, develop strong interpersonal and communication skills, build a circle of friends and find the courage to walk away from "frenemies," set boundaries, and handle the pervasive influence of social media.

Finally, Part 3 focuses on a girl's journey onward in the world. It provides ways to help her connect with her higher purpose and passion, stay motivated, make healthy decisions, and use feedback and failure as opportunities to strengthen and grow.

help her connect with her higher purpose and passion

During the preteen years, she will most likely learn these lessons at school, which is like a girl's job, but the lifelong habits of curiosity and working hard will serve her long after graduation. Part 3 also discusses ways to inspire her to see beyond herself toward her family, community, and society, and the endless ways she can make a real difference in the world, starting right now.

Growing Strong Girls is meant to encourage you when you feel you aren't doing enough, to inspire you with fresh ideas and perspectives when you feel you've run out of them, to equip you with information and relatable stories, to motivate you to action, and to convey to you that YOU CAN DO

Inspire her

IT!—even though some days it can feel like one step forward, three steps back. It *is* possible to raise girls to be strong, and small, incremental steps toward this will have profound and long-lasting effects on a girl's life.

This book is also meant to serve as the bridge between information about girlhood and the practical, step-by-step guidance girls need. Because I want to facilitate your connection and help you start conversations that actually go somewhere, at the end of each chapter you'll find a "Cultivating Connection" box, with discussion prompts and ideas for activities you can do together to drive home the ideas in that chapter and really bring them to life. In addition to the Cultivating Connection boxes, there are several "Connection Tools" throughout the book, such as a list of ten simple ways to connect, and a list of emotions to facilitate talking when feelings get overwhelming. There are even more resources gathered together at the back of the book, including positive power statements, my best homework and studying tips, and a list of common concerns I hear from parents, along with ideas for addressing them. I also suggest books and online resources you may want to use, either together with the girl in your life or for personal research and inspiration—look for the "Read More" sidebars in every chapter.

Truth telling also teaches girls to be honest with themselves

As well, you can join the Growing Strong Girls movement by using the hashtag #growingstronggirls via Twitter, Instagram, Facebook, Pinterest, and Snapchat. You can also visit me online at www.LindsaySealey.com, where you will find downloadable materials, videos, podcasts, and blog posts from me. We have an accessible community for further support, advice, ideas, and inspiration. We adults need connection too.

Along the Way

As you explore these discussions and activities, keep two things in mind. First of all, a girl needs to know that although she may not get what she wishes for, she will get what she works for. Being strong, like any skill we desire to develop, takes practice—each and every day. And this takes patience (she won't always get it right the first time) and perseverance (she will have to be determined in her decision to be strong). Likewise, growing strong girls doesn't *just happen*. We need to be intentional about it and committed to our decision.

Second, it is our responsibility to tell girls the truth. Be honest about who they are: what you see as their core strengths, but also the things they can work on. With acceptance of the truth comes the liberty to plan next steps. Truth telling empowers girls and encourages inner strength; truth telling also teaches girls to be honest with themselves.

Sometimes girls need advice, ideas, and help, but more often than not, they need time, presence, undivided attention, and non-judgmental listening. Girls are actually pretty talented at solving their own problems if we provide them with the safe space to do so. What I am proposing in this book is the *Strong girls become strong women.* same thing I do with my company Bold New Girls: merging social and emotional learning with academic success, which is how we empower girls to view and navigate the world through a positive lens and in a positive way. To equip them to make healthy choices that contribute to their sense of fulfillment, belonging, and purpose. Strong girls become strong women when they accept and love who they are, are proud of all they have accomplished and all that they are, embrace ongoing growth and development, and have clarity and life purpose.

Let's learn to cultivate connection so you can journey alongside your girl as she connects deeply inward with her true self, healthily outward in relationship with others, and boldly onward in the world. Connection begets connection, so the more time you spend with her, the more supported she will be to make these connections for herself. That's the key to growing strong girls.

A Note to Readers

GROWING STRONG GIRLS is intended to offer research, experience, and strategies to help you connect with and journey alongside girls. It is not intended to be a replacement for professional medical advice. Anyone who is truly struggling needs and deserves guidance customized to their specific needs.

Holding children in secure connection includes listening to and honouring what makes them unique and what they need as they grow. This book is intended for readers who care for girls ages nine to fourteen, but with some modification, you will find that the ideas and activities facilitate connection with many age groups. Furthermore, everything in this book was conceived for girls with a variety of levels of ability, from different ethnic, cultural, and religious backgrounds, and who may have non-traditional gender identities. For the purpose of consistency, I use the pronouns "she" and "her" throughout. Language grows and shifts over time—though sometimes not as quickly as the pace of social change. The qualities strong girls possess will one day enable them to lead these evolving conversations about inclusivity.

I present true stories in this book but have changed all names and identifying details to protect the privacy of the individuals and families involved.

Lastly, I want to underline that it is the responsibility of adults to keep the children in their care safe. If you feel any child is in danger, or is endangering another, please take action immediately and seek professional help.

PART ONE
A Girl's Journey Inward

Growing Strong by Connecting Inward to the True Self

THE MOST IMPORTANT relationship a girl will ever have is the one she develops with herself. When we prioritize making a solid connection with her, she can know, first-hand, what a secure relationship feels like, and she can emulate that security as she looks at her whole self: her emotional, mental, social, physical, psychological, and spiritual aspects.

When a girl knows who she is, she is empowered with the self-knowledge to grow strong; when a girl recognizes how she is feeling in the moment, she is empowered with the self-awareness necessary to be strong.

Think about it: Who knows all her favourite things? Who knows what she fears most? Who knows her deepest, darkest secrets and her magical, adventuresome dreams? Who knows how to love her and be there for her in the exact ways she needs? Who knows how to provide the kindness and self-compassion she needs at exactly the moment she needs it? The answer to all these questions is: she does.

A girl requires courage to connect with her true self. It takes fierce boldness to look inward and to really see all she is with acceptance and love—both the parts she is proud of and the parts she feels tempted to hide. It takes real fortitude and bravery to embrace her uniqueness in a culture that is begging her to conform. A girl's strong sense of self and her rich inner life become the solid foundation on which she can navigate her journey outward in relationships with others and onward in her life and work, and cultivate a desire to shape the world in which she lives.

We can encourage this growing connection inward by guiding her to spend time figuring out who she is and trusting that everything she needs she already has deep within herself. It is through sitting in stillness that a girl's greatest source of strength and inner power becomes heightened. We can be the support she seeks by seeing her and hearing her. We can reflect back the worth we see in her, and be the gentle reminder of how valuable she is—valuable not because of how others see her but just as she is.

I   Who I Am

"I KNOW *EXACTLY* who I am," said the seven-year-old sitting across the table from me. Maya and I were working on an exercise I call "All about Me," and she was right: her answers to my questions such as "What are your favourite things?" and "What are you really good at?" came flying out of her mouth so quickly, I had trouble keeping up with her. She was beaming brightly and loving the attention she was garnering from me. I couldn't help but think, "This is one confident girl!"

A girl's number one job is to get to know the girl in the mirror and who she is, really. This might be as simple as knowing her favourite breakfast cereal or choosing her own outfits for school, and as complex as her intuitive sense of how she feels each and every day and what makes her feel most happy and authentic. When girls know who they are, they are more confident and clear, which naturally extends to their making healthy choices for themselves. A girl who knows who she is will know what best meets her needs and, at the same time, she will start to learn what doesn't. She can recognize what feels aligned with her values and what feels out of alignment or wrong. It's when girls are around the age of nine that I've seen many of them slip out of alignment, lose touch with their self-knowledge, and become distracted by new pressures from peers and the world at large, or discouraged by adversity. Self-knowledge provides clarity and security for the challenges and uncertainties ahead.

We can help a girl know who she is and be who she is by encouraging her to take time each and every day to consider two questions: Who am I? and Who do I want to be? This time to be still, reflect, and connect with herself is very important; a girl cannot gain self-knowledge amid noise and chaos. A girl's connection with herself begins with our getting to know her and then extends into our showing her how to get to know herself. We can help her connect more deeply and authentically with herself by nurturing her own vulnerability and by encouraging her to see and to live her authentic truth.

"We are all gifted in a unique and important way. It is our privilege and our adventure to discover our own special light." MARY DUNBAR

A growing girl may encounter "stuck points," where she feels she isn't growing, and she may become narrowly focused on one aspect of knowing who she is, such as her appearance. This is when we can encourage her to navigate life in an open-minded and open-hearted way and remind her that knowing who she is is an ongoing process—she will always be in an eternal state of "becoming." As poet and storyteller Sarah Kay says to her imaginary daughter, and to every girl, "You are the girl with small hands and big eyes who never stops asking for more."[1] I feel that this quotation captures the idea of ceaseless wonder and the childlike openness for "more."

I want a girl to know that the more open she is to all ideas and all possibilities, the more fully she can come to know all the details about her authentic self. I want a girl to know that being open-hearted and vulnerable can further help her to grow into who she wants to be, and that being strong doesn't mean never being vulnerable—in fact, the opposite is true. Being vulnerable means exploring her hopes, dreams, and aspirations; daring to be inspired; and taking risks to be whom she really wants to be.

"Vulnerability is the core, the heart, the center of meaningful experience." BRENÉ BROWN

Although the world is big and the future can seem scary, any time she invests in really getting to know herself is time invested in her ability to handle whatever the future brings her way. Repetition and continuous practice should be a priority for a girl who is just beginning to figure out her inner self. Knowing, then loving, herself can take time, so she needs to start now. And this is where you come in; you have the privilege of starting these amazing conversations with her about her favourite things, the ways she describes herself, and who she hopes to be.

Guiding a girl to be strong and rooted in who she is allows her to feel her burgeoning inner confidence, security, and wholeness. With a clear and solid sense of self, a girl can move through life with inner strength. A girl won't stay seven forever, but we can continue to protect and nurture the shining seven-year-old confidence in each and every girl as she grows up.

CULTIVATING CONNECTION

Let's talk about:
- What she likes and dislikes.
- Some of her favourite things.
- What she feels she is good at. What she is growing in.
- What she is most proud of. What she is worried about.

Let's try:

- Creating an "All about Me" poster. In the middle of the poster, ask her to draw herself or print "Me." Then ask her to print, all over the poster, words and phrases that describe herself, using markers of different colours.* Ask her to consider favourite things, hobbies, interests, likes, dislikes, qualities, dreams, and goals. If she gets stuck, help out with prompts such as *How does your teacher describe you?* or *How do you think your friends see you?* or *What do you like doing on a Saturday?*

- Encouraging a variety of interests and skills. Expose her to several different opportunities; part of knowing who she is includes knowing what she likes and doesn't like. Play up personal strengths and play down competition and comparing.

- Teaching her to practise positive power statements such as *I can solve this problem if I just keep trying* and *I know I am smart enough and strong enough to do what I want.* She learns to accept herself and what happens to her when she can say, *I know I didn't have a great game, but I really appreciate how I played with determination* or *I love how I show bravery, even when I feel scared.*

*Whenever I suggest activities that invite you to create materials together, always feel free to use a range of colours, which is beneficial because colour is processed by multiple parts of the brain. Different colours may stimulate different brain functions (creativity, focus, attention, relaxation, critical thinking, and memory) and help with pattern recognition.

READ MORE
The Gifts of Imperfection, by Brené Brown

VIEW MORE
"If I Should Have a Daughter," TED Talk by Sarah Kay

2   Being True to You

LET'S FACE IT, we live in the "land of sameness." Girls are inadvertently taught to strive for the same look, status, possessions, name brands, and achievements as others. (These norms vary from group of girls to group of girls, but they're always there in some form.) Why are magazines and social media sites such as Snapchat and Instagram so popular? Because being the same gives girls a sense of normalcy, and who doesn't want to feel normal? A sense of belonging and connection is a necessary ingredient for a girl's developing brain and sense of self. How does a young, impressionable girl honour her uniqueness and remain authentic in a society constantly pushing for conformity?

For girls to be their truest, most authentic selves, they need time to explore who they are, and time to become comfortable in their own skin. Authenticity—knowing yourself and being yourself—takes time and thoughtful reflection. Authenticity also requires the total truth: a girl needs to be able to tell herself the truth about who she is—*all* of who she is: the good, the bad, and the ugly. Yes, sometimes the task falls to us to dispel misconceptions she may have about herself—rip off the Band-Aid as gently as possible. I am sure you have struggled with insecurity and uncertainty about who you are (I know I have), or feeling like an imposter in your own life (especially when experiencing success); this makes you the perfect person to support her in figuring out how she can steer clear of being superficial or disingenuous.

Girls are beautiful when they exude inner confidence, security, and uniqueness, but girls' understanding of inner beauty is often overshadowed by expectations about outer beauty. Little girls see beauty in everything—butterflies, ballerinas, bubbles, and Barbies. But at age nine or so, their understanding of beauty often narrows, becoming defined by commercial standards, causing them to fixate on their bodies and obsess over their flaws or how they want their body to change, which often results in negative feelings about themselves.

"Who you are today . . . that's who you are. So be brave. Be amazing. Be worthy." SHONDA RHIMES

But who really should be the judge of what beautiful means? Social media and carefully crafted images used for marketing, or girls themselves? Let's ask her to shift her focus from externally defined beauty standards to her inner true beauty. Emphasizing true beauty begins with conversations about her inner qualities of being and uniqueness.

We can guide girls to be more inclusive about all aspects of themselves. I call this the "whole girl ideology," and it's one that encourages girls to see beyond their bodies to also consider their emotions, thoughts, and actions; their values, beliefs, and guiding principles. We must help girls become aware of the pressure of the world around them that pushes them to look a certain way, and help them understand that they don't have to give in to this influence. It will take time, but it's possible for girls to explore their inner qualities and how to develop these qualities even more. We must teach girls to embrace true beauty with self-love and self-acceptance.

To further develop authenticity, it's important to stop trying to be someone else. We can send girls the message "You do you!"

Many girls fall into the trap of acting a part; they begin to act the way they think others want them to act, motivated by a desire to be accepted and fit in. One day they are the "good girl" and "teacher's pet" in the classroom; the next, they're the "mean girl" to other girls on the playground or the "cool girl" around older girls. None of these parts is a true representation of the *real* girl underneath the surface. Being a "good girl" may actually be a source of inner conflict for a girl who really yearns to be her whole and authentic self, but feels she has to maintain the illusion in order to fit in and get that connection girls long for. On the other hand, being a "mean girl" may be a role a girl chooses to play, even though it may feel out of alignment with her values, because it seems like the only way to get a reaction and attention, thereby maintaining connection. For a further exploration of the good girl and the mean girl, see Chapter 15.

"I think that happiness is what makes you pretty. Period. Happy people are beautiful." DREW BARRYMORE

Acting takes a lot of work, and it's confusing to the girl herself and to others who don't know which persona they will encounter. This behaviour can cause her stress and promote feelings of disconnection with herself. Being fake is the opposite of being authentic, and it's a real turnoff when it comes to connecting socially. It is much less taxing and much more honest and genuine for her to be herself—consistently and authentically. And when a girl has the freedom to be her true self and trust herself, anything people say about her is useless noise that will not distract her or hold her back. A strong girl, learning to be herself, knows there will always be haters and those who try to make her feel insecure—but she has the power to simply turn down the volume.

READ MORE
The Body Image Workbook for Teens, by Julia V. Taylor

CULTIVATING CONNECTION

Let's talk about:

- Her uniqueness; what makes her different and special.
- Why it's important to be real and authentic.
- Why some people aren't authentic. Why they might choose to play a part.
- The harshness of comparative language, such as *She is so much smarter than I am.* Provide replacement language that both allows girls to be true to themselves and leaves them room to express how they're different from one another: *She is a top student in math, and I am strong in English.* Or, *Whether it's science or soccer, everything she tries seems to come so easily to her, and I know I am the type of person who needs more time and practice to develop my skill set.*

Let's try:

- Looking at a magazine together to find all the ways the girls pictured in it look the same (hair, makeup, clothes, bodies, facial expressions). Then ask her to consider focusing on her uniqueness. On a piece of paper, ask her to write the phrase "I am unique because..." and see how many ways she can complete the sentence.
- Choosing one idea of what makes her feel truly beautiful (this might be her kindness) and asking her to list the ways she demonstrates her kindness (helping her family, thinking

of her friends). Then ask her to spend the day purposely showing this quality and, at the end of the day, ask her how she feels about herself.

- Taking one day each week to have a "true beauty focus day." This means no "outer beauty" allowed. Take a day with no screen time, magazines, or advertisements. Ask her what she notices about her mood, her attention, her body, her thoughts, and her feelings.

CONNECTION TOOL
Ten Simple Conversation Starters

Sometimes conversations with girls can feel awkward, and they can definitely be tricky to start. Here are some ideas to help you get these conversations going.

1. I notice you...
2. I see that you are...
3. I appreciate when you...
4. I respect you for...
5. I hear you...
6. I am wondering what you think about...
7. I would love to hear your idea on...
8. I am so proud of you for...
9. I love you so much for...
10. I am impressed when you...

Perfectly Imperfect   3

PERFECTIONISM IS THE desire to be flawless and to accomplish one's goals without falling short of one's own high standards. Most of my clients have perfectionistic tendencies, which are obvious when they say things like "I'm never going to be good enough" and "I only got 95 percent on my test." They sit before me, erasing printing they see as not straight enough and relaying their busy schedules, and then tell me they are joining another team because it'll look good when they apply to universities. They push themselves beyond their boundaries. When asked to try something new—a quick drawing, say—they stare at me blankly. They freeze up not because they aren't competent, but because the idea of not drawing perfectly on their first try is so daunting to them that it's debilitating. Perfectionists are one "mistake" away from devastation.

Perfectionists are overly self-critical, and black-and-white thinkers. They are the achievers and hard workers who are always striving to improve. In short, perfectionists get the job done, and they exemplify excellence. Yet they are stressed out and incredibly hard on themselves. Perfectionists don't see the point in practice and process, only in perfect results. They can't value their efforts toward a desired outcome unless they achieve that outcome exactly as they imagined it. They crumble at the hint of criticism, and they shut down and refuse to try when they can't guarantee 100 percent accuracy. Perfectionism is often coupled with unhealthy BFFs, namely worry, anxiety, fear, and shame.

Girls especially can be their own worst critic. Ironically, many girls can't imagine being judgmental or deprecating to a friend. Often there's a striking juxtaposition between the language a girl uses toward a friend in need—"I told her she was going to be okay and that next time will be better"—and the language she uses to speak to herself—"I can't believe I totally screwed up!" Why is it so much easier to be compassionate toward a friend than toward oneself?

"It's okay that everything isn't okay all the time." TAYLOR SWIFT

So, why are girls so self-critical? Socialization is partly responsible. When girls see their friends being hard on themselves, they learn the language of self-deprecation. It's also a way to gain attention and empathy. When a girl is hard on herself, she can get instant support from other girls—although over time, this attention seeking can become annoying to others. Finally, girls can be tough on themselves because they don't consider alternatives. Tough love becomes second nature to them.

Perfectionists are shaped by many factors. Often, there's a push from home: high-achieving and successful parents often push their children (who receive the message, even if it's not clearly stated). There are many cultural influences too. Watch an hour of cable television, and you'll see a plethora of competition shows like *X Factor*, *Dancing with the Stars*, and *The Voice*, all based on selecting the "best" contestant and eliminating those who aren't "good enough." Social media isn't helping, with its steady stream of handcrafted shots of people's exciting, happy, and flashy experiences. We never get to see the shots that didn't make the post.

Perfection has its appeal: it's what we see all around us, and it's only natural to want a piece of it for ourselves. The pursuit of perfection is often equated with happiness, acceptance, and self-worth, so it might seem like a healthy path toward self-improvement.

Mostly, girls know that how they feel about themselves is a function of what they achieve and accomplish. If they please, perform, and perfect, they feel good about themselves—and their self-esteem increases. Conversely, if they don't please, perform,

"You've been criticising yourself for years and it hasn't worked. Try approving of yourself and see what happens." LOUISE HAY

and perfect (their sign of "not good enough"), they feel unhappy with themselves—and their self-esteem decreases.

Yet perfection doesn't exist. The idea of perfection is simply that: an idea. We have constructed this elusive concept, but its very core is neither real nor realistic. Girls think that if they just push a little more, and they try a little harder, *then* they will be perfect; but since this place called "perfect" doesn't exist, they never reach it. They simply try harder and push for more—perpetuating the destructive cycle that sounds like this: *If I just put a little more time and energy into looking, living, and being perfect, then I'll be loved and accepted. And when I feel "not good enough," I'll just put a little more time and energy into being "more" perfect.*

And because perfection doesn't exist, perfectionism is therefore based on illogical thinking. In the words of Brené Brown, a research professor in the field of social work, "Perfectionism is the belief that if we live perfect, look perfect, and act perfect, we can minimize or avoid the pain of blame, judgment, and shame . . .

it's a shield."[1] Perfectionism can be a shield for girls, protecting them from what they are afraid of: failure, rejection, judgment, and vulnerability.

> *"To be self-compassionate is not to be self-indulgent or self-centred. Treat yourself with love, care, dignity and make your wellbeing a priority."* **CHRISTOPHER DINES**

If we can deconstruct perfection for girls, we can help them embrace the healthy foundation of being "perfectly imperfect," where girls can see their uniqueness, areas of growth, things they are learning to do, and broken pieces as all parts of who they are. When coupled with their strengths, girls' imperfections make them authentic and whole. By helping girls let go of the idea of perfection and grab on to the idea of *personal best* instead, we can help them accept a new perspective. If girls can see that life is a series of mistakes and failures, along with successes and triumphs, they can enjoy the process and relax into life. This kind of understanding of ongoing development is filled with self-compassion and self-acceptance, in contrast to the all-or-nothing harshness of perfectionism.

This is why teaching girls self-compassion is paramount. Self-compassion is being kind and understanding with yourself, without judgment or criticism, at the very moment you need it. Self-compassion is a powerful way to discover inner happiness and emotional well-being. It might sound like this: *What a tough day. In this moment, I am experiencing discomfort. But, I can be here for myself and I can help myself through this difficult time. I am going to be okay!* Self-compassion is there for the taking no matter what is happening—it's there on good days and bad. It's not contingent on any kind of performance.

In her book *Self-Compassion: The Proven Power of Being Kind to Yourself*, Dr. Kristin Neff contends that self-compassion is the perfect alternative to self-esteem, because it "offers the same protection against harsh self-criticism as self-esteem, but without the need to see ourselves as perfect or better than others. In other words, self-compassion provides the same benefits as high self-esteem without its drawbacks."[2] Whereas self-esteem is about encouraging self-worth primarily through achievement, self-compassion says self-worth is unconditional because a person has worth on the inside, no matter what happens outside her.

According to Neff, self-compassion comprises three key components: First, self-kindness and the use of kind and gentle language when expressing a unique experience, especially in the face of difficulty or disappointment. Second, loving yourself with warm and caring self-talk and understanding that we all share a common humanity; for a girl, this means being able to see that, as "weird" as she feels as she grows and gauges how to fit in, she is more similar to other girls than she is different from them. And third, mindfulness—focusing on what is happening in the present moment, with less emphasis on the past or the future. Thanks to the research of Neff and others, people are beginning to see self-compassion as the essential tool it is.

You cannot tell a perfectionist to stop being perfect. She'll look at you like you're crazy. But you can encourage a perfectionist to slowly let go of big ideas of perfection and start shifting her focus away from a desired outcome and toward her real-life, real-time efforts. This means the emphasis is on working hard toward improvement and growth instead of on working hard for successful results and rewards. Self-compassion may just be the alternative for girls who are hard on themselves and self-critical, and who may disconnect when they experience a mistake or a moment of difficulty. By using self-compassion, girls can meet themselves where they are, simply noticing their efforts and accomplishments and refraining from self-criticism or focusing on what is left to do.

Chapter 6 explores mindfulness and will help you to help girls be more present and self-aware of sensory experience. Later in the book, when we look at social emotional learning (Chapter 21) and the growth mindset (Chapter 27), we'll explore the interconnection between learning, self-belief, effort, and a positive attitude.

You can infuse a perfectionist's journey with kindness and help her recognize her growth and progress. And you can guide a perfectionist to see perfectionism as a gift—and if she can open her special gift, she can see all the lessons in perfectionism, there to be explored and to help make her feel less stressed out and stronger.

CULTIVATING CONNECTION

Let's talk about:

- What it means to be "perfect," and whether she thinks perfection is a healthy goal. (Girls often associate perfection with feeling happy, being accepted, and being well liked by others.)
- The benefits of perfectionism (high standards, achieving goals, determination, hard work, effort, and achievement) and the drawbacks of perfectionism (stress, worry, anxiety, black-and-white thinking, feeling "not good enough," and feeling that if she can't be the best at it, she doesn't want to try at all).

- Self-compassion and what it might mean to her: How would she feel if she was able to be there for herself, without judgment? Explain how self-compassion is a quality inside of her, to be used whenever she needs it.

Let's try:
- Practising a new skill together that neither of you has tried before, and giving each other permission to have fun and not worry about how good you are at it. Think a beginner's class in drawing, pottery, hip-hop dance, or jewellery making.
- Celebrating your own mistakes as teachable moments. Pause to notice, then explain, that you made an error and now you are ready to learn and grow. This helps her to see that you make mistakes too, and that mistakes can be positive experiences.
- Practising using the phrase "good enough" throughout the day. For example, make cookies together, and instead of trying for perfectly round cookies, focus on "good enough" shapes. Focus on enjoying the process more than on achieving the finished product.
- Preparing for self-compassion: Take a jar or box and spend some time filling it with ideas of how she can be there for herself when she needs to be. Using small pieces of coloured paper, fill the jar or box with ideas, for instance, *A self-hug, A time out*, and *Telling myself I will be okay*. Then, when she has a moment of difficulty or is using negative self-talk, remind her that she can look at these ideas and choose which one she wants to try out.
- Asking her to imagine what she would say to her friend if that friend were having a bad day. Explain to her that she

READ MORE
The Gifts of Imperfection, by Brené Brown

No Body's Perfect, by Kimberly Kirberger

Nobody's Perfect, by Ellen Flanagan Burns

Self-Compassion: The Proven Power of Being Kind to Yourself, by Dr. Kristin Neff

VIEW MORE
"Perfectionism,"
by Dr. Kristin
Neff, self-
compassion.
org/category/
exercises/

can also say those things to herself when she is having a bad day. In the same ways that she might be there for her friend, she can be there for herself.

Self-Care and
the Whole Girl 4

YOU ARE READING this book because you care. And you demonstrate your care in many ways, from providing for your daughter's basic needs for food and clothing to delivering comfort and emotional safety. As girls grow up, consider shifting from *care giver* to *care guider*. Empower girls to demonstrate that they can care for themselves, deeply and deliberately, as they grow up. You will be the best judge of how to balance providing care with encouraging her self-care.

So see what happens when she learns how to practise self-care and self-nurture and realizes that she can ease her stress and discomfort, feel more confident, and discover more pleasure and fulfillment in her days. There are many ways to encourage a girl to turn inward and provide herself with the care she needs and deserves. As girls take the lead in identifying their needs and getting them met, they learn invaluable life lessons of independence and responsibility.

When girls come to know how to provide for themselves, they send a clear message to themselves (and others) about their self-worth and self-respect. This can be revolutionary. They will have to come to terms with the fact that putting one's own needs first will inevitably mean disappointing those who are used to a different status quo. Girls are natural caregivers and nurturers, but often their priorities become skewed—for example, when they help a friend in need even though they themselves feel depleted and empty. By making the decision to care for herself first, and until she feels restored, she will ultimately have more to offer others.

Girls need to know that self-care is not selfish. Rather, it's a gift they can give to themselves. And when girls make self-care a habit and choose to focus on self *first*, they may feel enhanced inner strength, emboldened to keep going, and as though they can conquer the whole world!

"Conversations require complete disregard for the clock." JULIA ROBERTS

Self-care is a daily and consistent habit, a reflective practice of knowing and loving the entire self. Getting started can be as simple as choosing to do even one good thing for herself every day. Let's look at self-care in terms of the whole girl: physical, mental, emotional, and spiritual.

Physical Self

Girls taking care of their bodies begins with excellent hygiene. This includes washing their body, cutting their nails, brushing their hair, and caring for their skin with sunscreen, medicated cream, and moisturizer.

Beyond these hygiene basics, we need to educate girls to honour and respect their bodies by fuelling and nourishing them with whole and nutritious foods and drinking plenty of water to stay hydrated. The expression "You are what you eat" is absolutely correct! When girls eat healthy foods such as fruits, vegetables, lean proteins, and whole grains, and limit sugary, fatty, and processed foods, not only will they have more energy, but they will feel healthier and better about themselves. Consuming nutritionally dense foods will contribute to healthy, glowing skin, strong teeth and nails, and thick and shiny hair, not to mention more balanced hormones (helpful to avoid painful periods) and emotions (fewer mood swings).

We can embolden girls with the eating philosophy "Eat when hungry, and stop when full," or author Michael Pollan's good advice for healthy eating: "Eat food, not too much, mostly plants."[1] If a girl can connect to and be mindful of the feedback from her body, she will gain wisdom about what kind of self-care she needs. It's important that she knows that her weight does not determine her self-worth.

One need that girls sometimes underestimate is that of keeping active and moving their bodies every single day to stay fit and healthy. Being physically active aids in digestion, disease prevention, stress reduction, and mental performance and productivity. As well, girls who are physically active are more likely to have confidence and a healthy body image. Physical exertion throughout the day will also improve sleep, and sleep is a nonnegotiable necessity: they need at least eight hours each night to restore and rejuvenate. Getting adequate sleep will improve memory and creativity (and grades), build focus and attention, and, again, increase positive moods. A girl has a plethora of activities to choose from—indoor or outdoor, solo or group—and she may want to explore numerous options to find out which she loves most, and which is the best fit for her level of physical ability.

Ultimately, girls need to know that their bodies know exactly what to do and how to achieve wholeness and balance. It's their job to pay attention, listen, and trust in their bodies, and then to get out the way so their bodies can keep them healthy.

Mental Self

As girls grow, their brains continue to grow too (until age twenty-four). We can teach girls how to care for their brains and not just by wearing helmets when they bike. We can teach girls how to manage their thoughts. It's not easy to become aware of what you're thinking and to self-regulate a busy mind—for any of us at any age! Girls need to understand the maxim "Don't believe everything you think." Thoughts will come and go like monkeys swinging from branch to branch (the "monkey mind" is a common metaphor in certain schools of meditation), but they don't need to believe them all. We can encourage girls to investigate their thoughts, releasing any that keep them stuck, by teaching them to first pay attention and to then be curious about their thinking, with questions such as "Is this thought true?" and "How do I know it is true?"

I can tell you that as girls' brains develop, they start to gain what we call "metacognition," the ability to think about their thinking. As metacognition develops, girls can improve their awareness of *what* they are thinking and to what *degree*. It's true—sometimes girls' thoughts are bang on, and can be trusted to guide them to the right decision; other times they are inaccurate or exaggerated. We can help girls sort through their thoughts until they learn to do it themselves. But we'll never be able to help them do this if we aren't cultivating connection and talking with them on a regular basis—how else will we know what thoughts keep coming up for them?

Girls greatly benefit from stress-reduction activities such as deep breathing, muscle relaxation, and visualization, to slow down and calm their rapid-fire thinking—or, as I call it, their A-to-Z thinking—and to focus on one thought at a time.

Emotional Self

We can help girls care for their emotions by encouraging them to express themselves. So many girls keep their feelings hidden and buried inside. We can teach them that their emotions can seem much worse and larger when kept on the inside, and convey to them the importance of sharing their inner worlds. Holding feelings inside can negatively influence girls' physical health and well-being. We can encourage girls to explore their feelings with us. Often, when girls are given the safe space to do so, they feel unburdened and restored. If girls aren't comfortable confiding in a trusted friend or family member, they might seek alternatives, such as writing in a journal, drawing or colouring, meditation, or yoga.

"Many of the most accomplished girls are disconnecting from the truest parts of them-selves, sacrificing essential self-knowledge to the pressures of who they think they ought to be." RACHEL SIMMONS

Girls need to learn that when they can identify their feelings and express themselves freely, they are caring for their needs and are much more likely to feel relieved, supported, and like they are not alone. It's also important for girls to be able to match their emotional needs appropriately. By that I mean, if a girl can identify that she is sad, she can get her needs met with a hug or a safe space in which to release her tears, for instance. Conversely, if a girl is feeling happy, she can get her needs met by excitedly telling you all about her amazing day.

Sometimes emotional needs are met in unhealthy or avoidant ways—being angry with the wrong person, or taking a vow of silence and refusing to talk. Worse yet is when girls look for such extreme disconnection that they self-harm. Self-harm is a way for girls to manage uncomfortable and painful feelings. It can relieve built-up emotions, reduce stress, and help girls feel numb so that they "don't have to feel anything," especially emotional pain. Self-harm can also be a way to ease social anxieties, or even to retaliate against those who have wronged her. Self-harm is an external indicator of an internal struggle and a blatant cry for help.

Self-harm is an effective behaviour insofar as it provides short-term relief, but it comes with negative long-term consequences. By the time a girl engages in self-harm, she is desperate and may feel she has no other option. Self-harm can take the form of cutting or burning skin, scratching, binge drinking or excessive drug use, or an eating disorder. (If you suspect that a girl is participating in extreme self-harm, please seek professional help.) More subtle forms of self-harm include emotional eating, social isolation and withdrawal, harsh self-criticism or perfectionism, and self-neglect, such as ignoring personal hygiene. All these behaviours have one thing in common: they are seen as superior alternatives to feeling unbearable emotional pain.

A recent—and startling—discovery by sociologists is that a proliferation of online chat rooms for girls who participate in self-harm has shifted self-harm from a psychological disorder to a subculture that involves exploring how to harm oneself "better." With this shift, self-harm took on new social meanings, remaining a behaviour practiced by psychologically troubled individuals who used it to soothe their trauma, but also it became a legitimated mode of emotional expression and relief among a wider population."[2] As I see it, the insidious potential of the Internet to encourage harmful behaviour is just another reason girls need you to spend time with them face to face.

Whatever form self-harm takes, we need to see this subculture as one demanding our attention and intervention. Girls are not the problem here; the problem is the problem. Something is wrong, and there are reasons behind this extreme, devastating form of disconnection. As the supporters of girls, we must figure out the *why* that is driving these destructive behaviours, so that we can assist them in getting the help they need and in ultimately making healthier choices. Self-harm is a clear marker that strong needs—usually coping tools and, specifically, self-care—are not being met. Self-care, then, is the preventive approach to self-harm.

Let's rewind. Take the girl who has had a terrible day: she is rejected by a boy and called a disparaging name like "bitch" or "slut"; she feels as if her life has gone from bad to worse. Devastated, she returns home from school, only to find her parents both working late again and none of her friends responding to her texts. She resorts to cutting because she wants to numb out, but also because she feels that nobody cares, so why should she?

How can we prevent her from getting to a place of such despair? A focus on self-care may not prevent all acts of self-harm, but foundational work on the front end can drastically decrease the likelihood of the destructive behaviour and illuminate alternative paths to managing difficult feelings and practising self-care.

Spiritual Self

A girl's spiritual self can mean many things, but mostly it is the connection she feels with herself and the world around her. A girl's spirituality moves far beyond her daily activities of school, sports, and friendships. To encourage girls to take care of their spiritual selves, and their inner peace and joyfulness, we can discuss the importance of quiet time and of time alone for self-reflection. This means slowing down, making and taking time to be still, and removing all distractions from sight (smartphones, iPads, laptops). It is in these quiet moments of solitude that girls can consider who they are and how they want to contribute to the world. As it says in the Bible, "In quietness and trust is your strength."[3] We can facilitate spiritual growth in girls by helping them explore the ways they can foster this growth. This could be time spent outside, time spent alone, or time spent with a higher power. When girls become centred and grounded in themselves and care for their innermost being, they feel strong and stable in a new way. Chapter 10 examines girls and spirituality in more depth.

As you have read, care comes in many ways, and it can be nurtured and taught from a very young age. When a girl comes to practise self-care on a daily basis, she feels she is worth caring for, and this will help her be clear about her value and about how others must value her too. A girl who understands and embraces self-care habits understands that she can take care of her needs and respect herself, and that self-care is self-love. We can definitely tell her when she is displaying wonderful self-care, and we can step in when she needs a few hints about how she could do a better job of caring for herself.

CULTIVATING CONNECTION

Let's talk about:
- Why self-care is so important.
- All the different ways to practise self-care and the different ways to nurture her body, mind, and soul. There are many possibilities. And don't forget about the simple things she can do, like drinking lots of water, adding special requests to the family grocery list, and keeping in her backpack things like tissues for a runny nose, lip balm to heal dry lips, lotion for soothing dry skin, and Band-Aids (just in case). Other ways include listening to inspirational music and watching inspirational movies.

- How practising self-care could make her feel. Have her say these positive messages out loud and explain how it feels when she tells herself *I am worth it, I deserve care,* and *I love how I feel when I take care of myself.* Is it difficult for her to accept that these are all true?
- What you notice: *I notice that you seem sad lately. I notice that you seem quiet. When you are ready, let's talk about these feelings.* Use a light yet caring tone; you won't get anywhere if you sound critical or accusatory.

Let's try:
- Creating a self-care package for when she feels she needs extra comfort and care. Find a container and spend some time gathering items she feels she can use to care for herself, especially those that engage the senses. Think about including chewing gum, a hair brush, lip balm, and hand lotion.
- Creating a self-care plan, listing as many ideas as possible for self-care acts she can practise throughout the day, such as using an umbrella when it rains, giving herself a self-hug or pat on the back, or holding a key chain or memento that reminds her of you. Decorate the self-care plan; laminate it if you're able.
- Experimenting with various foods, and asking her to gauge how she feels when she eats certain foods (for example, a handful of candy versus a handful of nuts and raisins), to teach her the difference between foods that drain and foods that fuel.
- Having a pamper night of washing hair, experimenting with hairstyles, cleaning and polishing nails (hands and feet), soaking and moisturizing feet, and mini-massages. Throw

READ MORE
The Art of Extreme Self-Care, by Cheryl Richardson

The Tender Cut: Inside the Hidden World of Self-Injury, by Patricia Adler and Peter Adler

VIEW MORE
U.S. Department of Health and Human Services, www.girlshealth.gov/

in a movie you both love and a bowl of popcorn and it'll be even more fun!

- Creating a sleep-time ritual: consider preparing for bed with a shower or bath, fresh pyjamas and bedding, warm lighting, candles or a scent (perhaps an aromatherapy diffuser with essential oils), and either a book to share with her or a conversation about her day and anything on her mind. This ritual might become something she starts to look forward to—a winding down from her busy day, and a time to feel nurtured and calm.

CONNECTION TOOL

Self-Care—Ten Ways to Feel Good about You

Self-care can be easy to talk about; the hard part may be doing it. So here are 10 ideas to for putting self-care into action.

1. Drink enough water.
2. Get enough sleep.
3. Eat a variety of whole and nutritious foods.
4. Spend time with people who help you to feel good.
5. Have fun and laugh.
6. Practise life balance.
7. Speak kindly and positively to yourself.
8. Set boundaries and stick to them.
9. Make time for YOU!
10. Do more of what makes you happy.

Girl in the Mirror 5

WOULDN'T IT BE amazing if girls looked in the mirror and just smiled at what they saw? Girls are exceptionally good (as are most women) at pointing out and highlighting their bodies' flaws, what they don't like and what they feel they need to change. Isn't it heartbreaking to watch her critique her beautiful body and wish she were someone else? We need to inspire our girls to be kind to their bodies, and kind to themselves.

When times get tough and they need to regain a sense of control, girls can turn on their bodies, blaming and denying. As counsellor Julia V. Taylor says, "When you try something that doesn't work and you can't figure out why, it's easy to turn your insecurities into body blaming because your body is right in front of you."[1] The body itself is not the problem, but by focusing on weight and other aspects, a girl can manufacture a feeling of control to distract herself from the feeling that her world is spinning out of control. This strategy may give a girl a temporary sense of relief and an elusive sense of control and sense of self, but in the long term, this strategy may contribute to her damaging her body and neglecting her true need for body love and connection.

We can help girls, before they turn against their bodies, to have a true and honest relationship with them. As we saw in Chapter 4, this means nourishing themselves with nutritious foods, hydrating with a lot of water, being active and exercising, and resting and rejuvenating. It also includes speaking kindly and positively toward herself. When a girl feels out of control, it is a sign for her to amplify her self-care, not turn against herself. When it feels like the world is spinning out of control, she can take that as a sign that she needs to take better care of herself, not neglect herself. Encourage her to look with soft and loving eyes at her body and at those around her, instead of with critical eyes.

> *"I keep telling myself that I'm a human being, an imperfect human being who's not made to look like a doll, and that who I am as a person is more important than whether at that moment I have a nice figure."* EMMA WATSON

And that will be a challenge, given that girls are constantly bombarded by the media's subliminal messages that they are not good enough, not beautiful enough, not skinny enough. They see as many as three thousand images each day and are growing up with such advertising as an integral part of youth culture.[2] Many of these ads are designed for the sole purpose of selling products, labels, ideas—all of which involve skewed notions of happiness, success, and perfection. Even #nofilter posts—the current trend—are deceptive, since, in reality, achieving this "effortless appearance" requires a great deal of effort.

To guide a girl in developing a positive and healthy body image, teach her to focus on what she loves about her body—in terms of both how it looks and what it can do. Ask her what these things are. She may say her beautiful blue eyes or her shiny hair or her high jumping or her ability to run long distances or swim like a fish. Let her choose. The point is to switch her focus from finding flaws to seeing the beauty of what she's got.

Encourage her to look at the real bodies of others—this means girls at school, not models on the runway or the pages of magazines. Girls seem to be eager to let go of being little girls and skip ahead to adolescence and, yes, being sexy. It may start harmlessly, playing dress-up and wearing Mom's heels, singing along to pop songs that describe the experiences of young women. Eventually, the everyday outfits growing girls choose may become inappropriate (hiked up really high or slung really low) and their makeup more noticeable, and before they know it, they're beaming with pride at the comment that they are "hot."

Girls equate "hot," "pretty," and "sexy" with being accepted; they aren't equating looking sexy with the actual act of sex. Risqué outfits may be trendy, but these clothing options tend to attract unwanted attention. Because of changes in diet and exercise (and an accompanying increase in body mass index, or BMI), girls are maturing physically faster and earlier than those of any other generation; girls as young as eight are wearing A cups and have clear curves. This does not mean their emotional maturity matches their bodies, nor that they understand the social and emotional damage that might result from dressing sexily at such an early age.

It's not a girl's fault. Sex sells, and "sexy" content is everywhere—girls are inundated with graphic images, and they're being taught that being sexy is a valued quality in women. But I'd argue that most girls do not really want to grow up so soon. They want to play and have fun. They *think* they want to grow up quickly because of what they see in music videos and on social media. And they definitely want to be accepted. Sexual objectification can seem like a shortcut to connection, but it's a dangerous path—one that can ultimately lead to a much deeper sense of disconnection.

So let's encourage girls to stop obsessing over fabricated images of women they see in the media and to instead design images of their own. In my workshop "Media Madness and Mixed Messages," for girls ages nine to fourteen, I ask participants to identify mixed messages in magazines, including in the advertisements. It doesn't take them long. They point out headlines such as "Take the Perfect Selfie," followed by "Love Yourself Just as You Are!" Or "Be Your Best, Healthy Self" right beside "How to Lose Five Pounds in a Day." It also doesn't take them long to realize how confusing this could be for someone who doesn't know better. You don't need my workshop to teach girls to be skeptical of media messages. By being educated about the power of the media, girls will not only understand how the media is manipulating them, but also make the connection between what they see "out there" and how they feel on the inside. Once girls know this, they can't "unknow" it. This is the beauty of awareness.

The best tool with which we can equip girls is the truth, and here it is: There is nothing *wrong* with them. They are valuable just as they are. We need to teach girls that they are so much more than their bodies. Girls need to stop the comparison game. Each body is part of a larger, authentic, whole self. And there are aspects about each unique body that help to tell the story of who the girl is and where she came from. We can encourage her to dig deep within and accept whatever she discovers, including all the things that make her unique—her ethnicity, her culture, her gender identity, her abilities, and her disabilities.

Lead her to connect with her cultural and ethnic background as she notices and understands difference. Show her photos of her ancestors, so she sees that although her skin tone may not work with the shade of makeup her friends like to wear, it's exactly like her grandmother's. If she doesn't want to wear the same dress as the other members of her dance group, talk with her about why that is, and suggest ways to talk to her teacher about choosing her own costume.

Parents of girls with a physical disability or chronic illness are likely already aware of the value of accepting what bodies can do and what makes them beautiful. A girl must honour her unique features and appreciate body differences. And when people talk about her body—fat shaming, skinny shaming, or pointing out certain body parts or body changes—she needs to know that her body is her own and that these comments are not acceptable. She can push back by telling people that talking about her body is not okay!

"People often say that 'beauty is in the eye of the beholder,' and I say that the most liberating thing about beauty is realizing that you are the beholder. This empowers us to find beauty in places where others have not dared to look, including inside ourselves." SALMA HAYEK

Ask a girl to share her personality, and the qualities she feels she embodies, with you. Have conversations about hidden talents, strengths, and what she is learning to do. Be curious about her hopes and dreams and who she imagines becoming. Inner beauty—and nurturing a beautiful spirit—really does shine through and evolves into outer beauty. When a girl feels strong about her body and takes an inside-out approach to feeling and being beautiful, she is well on her way to understanding true beauty and the girl in the mirror.

READ MORE
The Body Image Workbook for Teens, by Julia V. Taylor

VIEW MORE
Killing Us Softly 4, Media Education Foundation Study Guide, by Jean Kilbourne

"Looks Aren't Everything. Believe Me, I'm a Model," TED Talk by Cameron Russell

CULTIVATING CONNECTION

Let's talk about:

- The body parts that she loves and the ones she doesn't love as much.
- How she feels in her body and when she is *moving* her body.
- What makes her feel the best in her body, and what makes her feel the worst.
- What she thinks "sexy" means.
- The three qualities that best describe who she is, and what outfits would best show these three qualities.
- The facts about advertising and the media businesses wanting to sell products, labels, and brands, with the ideas and feelings these entail; and the one-sided news stories we hear.
- How images are polished to perfection with techniques such as airbrushing, editing, and using Photoshop and filters. Consider experiment with Photoshop or other photo-editing software together.

Let's try:

- Creating a list of three things she loves about her body, and posting the list by her mirror, so that when she looks in the mirror, she will be reminded to focus on what she loves.
- Asking her to write a letter to her body, apologizing for any negative self-talk or neglect and expressing how she will take care of her body from now on.
- Eliminating comparisons between her and her friends or between you and her. Avoid using phrases such as "prettier than" or "skinnier than."
- Encouraging her to replace phrases like "I feel fat" with "I will care for my body by…"

- Inviting her to limit mirror time and screen time—there's a whole world out there!

- Helping her develop skills that are separate from her appearance. It's important she be well groomed, but it's equally important that her focus is on a skill set, such as a sport, art, music, theatre or schoolwork.

- Teaching her what to do when people comment on her body without her permission: a light response such as *You just focus on your body, I'll focus on mine* or a more direct response such as *Exercise helps me to cope with stress and anxiety, and I love it.*

- Checking out movies, TV shows, and magazines together. Ask her what she notices, and ask her to evaluate it. For example: *Do the models look like real people? Do they look like you and your friends? What do you think of their clothing? What does their "look" suggest about who they are? Do the characters show many qualities or just a few? How do you feel about what you see?* Let her do all the critiquing.

- Asking her to take the perspective of a boy she likes, a teacher, and her grandmother—how might each of them view a girl who posts a risqué photo of herself? See what answers she comes up with.

- Finding, together, role models whose physical appearance she finds appealing and who are doing great things to make the world a better place. For suggestions of positive role models, see Resource 6.

6   Mind Full to Mindful

THE GIRLS I work with often use phrases like "I feel so ADD." They're often not formally diagnosed, but they are searching for a way to describe their inner experience, and attention deficit disorder is a close fit. What girls are saying is that they are having trouble focusing and staying present in the moment. Their minds are *full*.

This is true not just for girls—we are all living in a busy, overwhelming, overstimulated era. We are a distracted society. Part of our busyness could be that there's too much on our minds and too many competing interests, but it's also avoidance of, and discomfort with, being in a moment—especially an awkward one. Most times, we are far from mindful, which means paying attention on purpose and practising a non-judgmental openness to new experiences.

When girls are distracted, there may be fidgeting, interruptions, quick changes of topics, and lack of eye contact. But often the signs of distractibility are much less obvious. Indeed, the underdiagnoses of ADD (attention deficit disorder) and ADHD (attention deficit hyperactivity disorder) in girls directly correlate with girls' ability to "look" like they are paying attention, all the while hiding a deeply troubled experience. According to *New York* magazine, the symptoms of ADD and ADHD can look different in girls than they do in boys (who tend to clearly demonstrate that they are distracted), in part because many girls do their best to hide them. Since a girl can present so masterfully and appear to be okay, even if what's going on inside her is a huge contributor to her distraction, nobody else may ever know, and she is likely to internalize what is happening for her as a personal flaw. And so, until recently, the signs of ADHD (daydreaming, disorganization, trouble following directions, and making careless mistakes on assignments and tests) have often been missed or dismissed in girls ("She's just absent-minded"). But according to a study in the *Journal of Clinical Psychiatry*, diagnoses of ADHD rose 55 percent for girls between 2003 and 2011. Among women ages twenty-six to thirty-four, ADHD prescriptions soared by 85 percent between 2008 and 2012 alone.[1]

But not all cases of distractedness are caused by ADD or ADHD. I was working with Elle, an eleven-year-old girl with an unrelenting enthusiasm for improving in school. We were focused on her executive functioning skills: time management, organization, planning, and preparation. She was improving and had mastered using her school planner to keep track of assignments and test dates. So it was a surprise to learn one day that Elle was no longer using her planner and failing to hand in assignments. Something was wrong and I was curious.

Now, my style of working with girls is not harsh or judgmental. I know the value of being on their side. And I could feel there was already conflict between her and her mom, and much disappointment for both of them. We started with a conversation about Elle's day and then about her week. With some gentle nudging, I learned the truth. Her agenda was not the problem. She "forgot" to use her agenda because she was distracted by the girls who didn't want to play with her at lunchtime. She was getting distracted because she kept thinking, "What's wrong with me?" and "Why don't the girls like me?" Those are pretty powerful thoughts, and they were a cause for concern—and a distraction for Elle. An agenda is not important at all when you are trying to figure out your place on the playground!

For girls like Elle, to be mindful means being aware of one's immediate experience *as it's happening*. This is a refined skill but a mandatory one. It can begin with being mindful of the body. When girls learn to do a body scan from head to toe (see Resource 7 for instructions) and check in with body signals such as hunger, fullness, hotness, coldness, soreness, and tension, they are using the gift of their body to know how to take care of their needs. Our

"By choosing to step forward consciously into the day, we can better appreciate each moment as it comes." GABRIELLE BERNSTEIN

bodies know exactly what we need (often before we are cognizant of those needs). Our bodies may subtly let us know when something is not right. For example, a slight feeling of hunger may mean we need food or water. If we don't pay attention to this sign, our stomachs start to growl, as if to scream at us, "Feed me now!" This is a direct and immediate experience. And by being aware of her immediate experience by paying attention to her body, she can know how to take care of it. In this example, she can choose nourishing food or water and restore her physical self.

Mindfulness is also about the mind (no surprise there!). Girls can overthink or ruminate. They spend a lot of time analyzing what was said to them, what they said, what they noticed, and what it all means. Like Elle, they become distracted by their thoughts. And although it's positive to be thoughtful and considerate, overthinking is tiring. We can help girls be mindful, starting with awareness. If we can encourage girls to ask the simple question "What's happening inside of me?" they can become more attuned with their inner experience and what, exactly, their thoughts are focused on. According to researchers of the MindUP program, developed by the Hawn Foundation, mindfulness is helping young people have better attention and more concentration, better interpersonal relationships, and the improved ability to manage stress and feel more optimistic.[2]

As girls become more aware of what they are thinking, we can guide them in what kinds of thoughts they have. Girls ask a lot of "What if?" questions—"What if I don't get invited to the party?" "What if I don't make the team?" "What if I don't get into university?" They often create their own stress with these anxiety-promoting questions. And when they talk about happiness, they use phrases like "I'll be so happy when I have more friends," and "I'll be happy when I finally get straight As," or "I'd for sure be happier if I was skinnier." So many ifs and whens.

For girls, often, happiness will be derived from an external source, at a future time, sometimes in an imagined or impossible set of life circumstances. They are constantly seeking happiness as if it's a destination, and they invest so much energy in the pursuit of the things, people, achievements, and accomplishments they think can get them there. All the while, they wonder why they feel empty, unfulfilled, and dissatisfied. It is in the search for happiness that they often miss out on the happiness right in front of them. And, of course, they never get to that happy place they are seeking, resulting in a constant cycle of searching yet never finding. Talk about frustrating.

With increased awareness, girls can acknowledge the present and even stop to say, "I am happy, right here, right now." The challenge for girls is to catch these fleeting moments, and they can do this only when they stop waiting for happiness. So what can we do to help? We must teach girls that happiness is in flux, coming and going as a series of moments, that it's a beautiful feeling they can choose to create right now, from the inside out, and learn to capture and savour; that it's not a single, magical destination, and that the choices they make can empower them. In essence, by learning how to capture happy moments and how to create more of them, girls can learn to cultivate their happiness.

We can help girls focus on the happiness available to them in the present moment by helping them develop new habits; habits that might include thinking of one way she can make someone else happy and then trying to find the opportunity to do it daily, or creating a list every night before bed of happy moments she experienced.

Girls can learn to define their own happiness and ask "What does happiness mean to me?"—as opposed to following celebrities' paths to "happiness." A girl's happiness plan should be designed by and unique to her, not taken from a generic magazine article titled "5 Ways to Boost Your Happiness." Further, if we teach girls that happy feelings can be generated by surrounding herself with "happy" influences—optimistic friends, inspiring music, and intriguing books and movies—they will start to discern between what is boosting and what is detracting from their happiness levels.

And we can help girls view unhappiness as a temporary state that they can step into and through, knowing that "this too shall pass." We can help girls plan for times of unhappiness by asking them to embrace it, then move forward when they are ready. The truth is we don't know what will happen next—all we know to be true is the reality of the present moment. More often than not, girls are okay in the present. So, if we can encourage girls to stick with the facts ("I know I tried my best," "I know I am a good friend"), they can focus on being in the moment and be more free to have fun and enjoy life. Self-created worry is a wasted emotion; it serves no purpose.

Finally, a hallmark of mindfulness is what is now being called "single-tasking." I know multi-tasking has become a source of pride for many people (of all ages). Girls constantly tell me how they can chat with friends online as they complete their homework. But dividing their time like this means that neither task gets done with the full attention required. For a girl, being in the moment and present means doing one task at a time—with full attention and effort—and then reaping the full rewards, not only for each project but for her brain, which can develop optimally.[3] The latest neuro-biological research points, though it might sound old-fashioned, to the value of completing one task before moving on to the next.

"If you're not happy during the journey, you won't suddenly be happy at the destination." LUCIE HEMMEN

Not only do tasks suffer from not receiving full attention, but the brain develops based on this as the norm and thus wires in ways that make future continuous deep focus on tasks impossible. Multi-tasking is a brain drain that exhausts the mind, zaps cognitive resources, and, if left unchecked, condemns us to early mental decline and decreased sharpness.[4] Chronic multi-taskers also have increased levels of cortisol, the stress hormone, which can damage the brain's memory region.

When girls fully engage in each task, they give themselves room to learn the power of observation. For instance, by observing what is happening as they eat lunch and how they feel as they eat lunch, they learn to connect themselves with the immediate experience of eating. They learn to calm down their feelings and thoughts, as well as their nervous and digestive systems, and be present. If a girl is playing soccer, she needs to play soccer. If she is on Instagram, she needs to pay attention to Instagram. If she is talking to her friend, she needs to talk to her friend. Full attention comes when girls can focus on single-tasking.

There is a clear connection between mindfulness, choosing to pay attention, self-care, choosing to care for oneself, and growing strong. As stated in an article on mindfulness by Kim D. Rempel, mindfulness may be the one helpful practice in addressing the stress and pressure of living in today's busy and overactive world.[5] When a girl focuses on being present and doing one task at time, she is caring for herself and helping her brain pay attention and be engaged. When girls learn to nurture their growing brains, they are also learning how to calm or regulate their brains and be strong as they move from mind full to mindful.

CULTIVATING CONNECTION

Let's talk about:
- Her busiest day, and what she notices when she is busy.
- The idea of mindfulness and slowing down her busy day to pay better attention to both herself and what is happening around her. Ask her what she can let go of today or in the week to help her feel less busy.
- The benefits of mindfulness, including feeling calm and relaxed, and being able to slow down to appreciate her experiences.
- What makes her happy, and how others might know that she is happy.
- What would make her feel even happier. What are some ideas to get there? (This is a great conversation starter because it both helps *you* learn what is concerning her and empowers *her* to take action.)

Let's try:
- Going for a mindful walk together. Choose a time that is good for both of you and take a short walk, during which you ask her to notice things, starting with her body—her

breathing, any sensations she feels, and feelings or thoughts that come up for her. Then ask her to shift to noticing with her five senses what is around her—what she sees, feels, hears, touches, and smells. You can guide her as you walk and ask questions, or you can ask questions beforehand and walk in silence.

- Practising mindful eating. Before a meal, take time to look at the food together. What colours does she see? What does she smell? Ask her to put some food on her fork, but instead of eating it, to bring it close to her mouth and smell it, noticing it. When she takes a bite, ask her what the food feels like and tastes like in her mouth. After she swallows, ask her to put down her fork and wait a moment before preparing for her next taste.

- Taking five minutes each day to sit together in silence (no devices!). Take slow, deep breaths, counting four seconds during the in breath, holding for four seconds, and counting four seconds during the out breath.

- Playing the "compliment catcher" game. Start by finding a fish net, kitchen strainer, or glass jar and then cutting up small pieces of coloured paper. Ask her to notice and remember all the compliments that come her way during the day. At the end of the day, ask her to recall and write down on the coloured papers each compliment, then gather the papers in the container. This game can also be used to record the compliments she gives.

- Creating a happiness plan for boosting her mood. Ideas on it might include blasting music and having a thirty-second dance party, quickly naming five of her happiest memories, going stargazing, skipping instead of walking, a short walk on which she's to notice five tiny things that make her

READ MORE
Mindfulness for Beginners, by Jon Kabat-Zinn

Mindfulness Workbook for Children, by Jenny Kellett

10 Mindful Minutes, by Goldie Hawn

What Happy People Know, by Dr. Dan Baker

TRY THIS APP
MindShift

happy, an "anything goes" dinner where she can choose to eat anything she wants (such as breakfast for dinner, or a bowl of sweets and treats), or time to think about what she is looking forward to.

See Resource 5 for a list of empowering songs that will put a smile on her face.

Life Balance 7

WHEN I THINK of life balance, I think of the foundational "mountain" yoga pose. In the practice of yoga, girls learn first and foremost to root their pose with both feet on the ground and to stand tall, anchored, steady, and strong.

This is how I see balance—when girls are balanced, they don't feel like they are leaning too far one way or the other. That is to say, they are not putting too much time or energy into any one activity or relationship. They don't spend too much time in stress mode or feeling overwhelmed. Conversely, they don't spend too much time in the land of boredom, feeling uninspired and disconnected from life. Balance means spending equal amounts of energy in many areas of life and feeling edified, whole, and content. This also means being diversified and learning as many new skills as possible.

When a girl is out of balance for too long, her health and happiness can suffer. Dr. Shimi Kang, author of *The Dolphin Way*, describes being out of balance: "If we ignore Mother Nature's guidance and don't pursue these activities (playing freely, exploring bravely, bonding socially, contributing wholeheartedly), we'll find ourselves off balance, and it will only be a matter of time before we fall over and get hurt. Our vitality, then our well-being, joy, self-motivation, and our health will slip away."[1] I agree with Dr. Kang. Many girls spend most of their time on schoolwork and are then devoid of time to rest and restore. On the flip side, many girls spend hours on social media and are then devoid of any self-motivation or ambition to do their homework. Both scenarios are examples of imbalance.

We can help girls achieve and maintain balance by encouraging them to explore what balance and vitality mean to them and, using principles of mindfulness, to explore how balance and vitality feel in the body. How does it feel to be balanced in the body? How does it feel to be balanced in life? Girls can learn to recognize when they come into balance, feeling aligned and in flow, and when they slip out of balance. Oftentimes, it's much easier to recognize how imbalance feels, which is an important lesson in itself. When girls learn to pay attention to what imbalance feels like—scattered, "off," wobbly, dizzy, out of sorts—they are better able to get themselves back on track by asking the essential question "What do I need to do to feel a better sense of balance?" and then seeking that out. Perhaps it's more sleep, more downtime, or more attention, or less processed food, being around fewer negative people, or having less on the to-do list.

"We can be sure that the greatest hope for maintaining equilibrium in the face of any situation rests within ourselves." FRANCIS J. BRACELAND

Life is busy and can be stressful; sometimes it's unavoidable to be temporarily out of balance. Girls need to get used to this because this is the reality of life. We can assist girls who are feeling out of balance by explaining to them that it's a temporary state. The key is building awareness about these temporary periods and how to lean into them, coming up with ideas about what they need to do to get back into balance—more self-care, a day off, some downtime to play, or help from a parent or friend.

No one can maintain balance constantly. We know the ideal state is anchored, steady, and strong, but this is not always the state in which girls find themselves. Just like yoga, it's a practice and an ongoing process of learning and growing. The rewards of life balance and alignment are numerous and foundational. And that's worth pursuing.

READ MORE
The Dolphin Way, by Dr. Shimi Kang

The Teen Girl's Survival Guide, by Dr. Lucie Hemmen

CULTIVATING CONNECTION

Let's talk about:
- Her schedule and what her typical day looks like.
- The idea of balance and spending time in all areas of her life (not just balancing school and time spent online, but also balancing alone time with friend time, school with play, FaceTime with "real" time).
- Whether she feels too busy, not busy enough, or the right amount of busy.
- Being too busy and how this can lead to stress and feeling overwhelmed. She may be too busy at certain times, but the goal is always to get back to balance. Talk about what that means for her.

Let's try:
- Taking a piece of paper and, with a pen, dividing it into four squares. Label the squares "Work/School," "Play," "Self," and "Others," respectively. Ask her to write down in each square all she does to contribute to that particular area. For example, the Work/School square might include notes about studying, doing homework, and math tutoring; and the Self square might include notes about reading,

Snapchatting, and brushing her hair. Encourage her to take her time with this. When she has finished, ask her to look at the squares to see which are "too full" or "not full enough." Ask her about doing "more" for some squares and "less" for others. The ideas she comes up with can be written on a separate sheet titled "New Ideas for Better Life Balance."

- Asking her to try the "flip the script" activity. This means planning a day when she does the opposite of what she normally does. For example, on her typical Saturday, she wakes up and eats cereal for breakfast; walks the dog, always taking the same route; and then goes straight to watching Netflix on her iPad. Create a plan that "flips" these typical Saturday activities so that the expected becomes the unexpected. She might eat pancakes for breakfast, take the dog somewhere new, and trade in her Netflix time for a crafts morning. She can always resume what she normally does, but the change-up—a day having some fun!—will serve as a reminder that change is a necessary part of balance.

Facing Anxiety   8

RECENTLY A MOM shared her story with me. Her daughter, Naya, was struggling at school: she was worried she wasn't going to make good enough grades to stay in her art program. Every Monday morning, Naya moaned and groaned and complained of stomach pains until her mother allowed her to stay home from school. Over time, Naya became more and more anxious each Sunday night. She was caught in a Sunday-night vortex of anxiety and avoidance. (Does this scenario sound familiar?) Eventually, Naya's mom realized how she was enabling Naya's daughter's behaviour.

Your daughter's anxiety may not be as deep as Naya's, but if she's ever asked you if she can leave school early or stay home from school because she feels "sick" on the day of a test, she was likely not lying; she probably *did* feel sick, but it was a sickness triggered by test anxiety.

Anxiety is a response to perceived danger. It's like an internal alarm alerting us to trouble in order to keep us safe. Anxiety is normal and common. It is absolutely necessary if there's a house fire, or if a stranger is walking too closely behind us. Anxiety is also healthy and helpful before a test or presentation, as it keeps us alert, focused, and prepared.

But too much anxiety can be crippling. When girls are stressed, their ability to absorb, retain, and recall information is inhibited. This is why urging them to study more before a test won't help. It's not uncommon for girls to study and know the material, only to blank during the test, then remember everything *afterward*. The blanking while writing a test is anxiety taking over. And when experiencing anxiety, girls may also feel fear, disappointment, anger, helplessness, or worry. They may have racing negative thoughts like "I'm so stupid" or "I'll never get the hang of how to write a test."

"I'm not telling you it's going to be easy. I'm telling you it's going to be worth it." ART WILLIAMS

Instead of letting this anxiety derail our girls, we can teach them that experiencing anxiety is a part of life that they can accept and manage. To do this, we first must teach girls to pay attention to the signs of anxiety, which means paying attention to their bodies. When girls are anxious, their bodies "rev up." Signs are different for each girl and may include a tight or turning stomach, sweaty palms, headache, muscle soreness or tightness, shallow breathing, and tiredness.

When a girl recognizes these clues, she can then acknowledge, "I'm aware I'm anxious." With awareness comes the natural next step of action, which is to take deep breaths and relax, to slow the body's systems so she is better able to focus on the sensory experience. She can ground herself in her sensory experience by focusing on what she sees, smells, and feels.

We can also help a girl pay attention to her self-talk, especially negative self-talk. Before a test, her telling herself "I'm going to fail" is only going to increase her anxiety. Rephrasing this statement as "I have studied, and I'll do my best" can generate feelings of calm and confidence. Or challenge her anxious thoughts with "What is your evidence that this thought is true?" Asking her to recall past experiences in which she felt anxious yet performed well—on a test or in any other situation—may help.

And sometimes asking "What is the worst-case scenario, and can you survive if that is the outcome?" is the best way to get her thinking positively again. (More on this strategy in Chapter 20, which explores how to turn setbacks into comebacks.) We can help a girl identify her anxious thoughts by asking her what she worries might happen. With this information, she can challenge her thoughts with kindness and self-compassion. She will then be able to walk herself through moments of stress by trusting that she does know *something*.

Finally, we can remind our girls that they can be there for themselves in times of anxiety, showing themselves compassion, and finding their sense of calm. A girl can remind herself to get back to her authentic self by using easy techniques such as deep breathing, muscle relaxation, and encouraging self-talk such as "I can do this" and "I've got this."

Even though many life events are beyond girls' control—life simply happens—a girl *can* control her perspective and her thoughts about an event or experience. This goes a long way toward managing anxiety. Can you imagine how this might feel for a girl, to know she has choice and power in her moments of anxiety? Let's say a girl's friend walks into the classroom but doesn't say hello to her, even though she always says hello. The girl cannot change the fact that her friend did not say hello. But what she thinks about it is fully within her realm of influence. She may think, "Oh no, what if my friend is mad at me and doesn't want to be friends anymore?" Then she may notice that her palms are sweaty, her breathing is shallow, and she is feeling anxious. This "What if?" question is a short but powerful one, and it's a big contributor to her anxiety.

Therefore, girls need to know that if they ask the negative "What if?" question, they also need to ask the positive "What if?" "What if my friend just didn't see me?" or "What if my friend has a lot on her mind this morning?" Both options are possible. And at least these two options can help the girl counter her first, negative thought. Or the girl may choose to focus on what she knows to be true, by countering the negative "What if?" question with a positive affirmation such as "I know I am a good friend, and I can be a good friend right now." (See Resource 2 for additional positive power statements.)

Both of these alternative strategies are effective because they help a girl have a choice in her anxious experience, and they promote calmness. Girls can practise being there for themselves in their anxious moments and showing themselves more self-compassion. They can then unburden themselves by sharing their anxiety and connecting with their emotions (and you) to gain a wider perspective. Once she's reached a calmer place and has the time to reflect, she can explore what triggers her anxiety response by asking questions like "What happened?" and "What am I thinking about what happened?" It is in this process of discomfort and reconnection to comfort that girls become stronger in their abilities to move *through* the difficulty, instead of turning away and feeling disconnected and alone.

CULTIVATING CONNECTION

Let's talk about:
- Anxiety and other words for anxiety, including "worried," "scared," "overwhelmed," and "nervous."
- That anxiety is normal and something everybody experiences (even you; she is not the only one).
- The ways in which anxiety affects her body, mind, and spirit.

- How anxiety can be a sign that something is not right, and how she can decide what she needs to do to manage her anxiety.
- How she can ground herself when feeling anxious by focusing on what she sees, hears, smells, and feels. Stress balls, decompression squeeze toys, magnetic steel balls, and sensory beads are great tools for promoting the sensory experience.

Let's try:
- Celebrating with her after her efforts and hard work. Praise her for having the courage to take tests; focus less on the results.
- Coming up with a list of triggers that might make her feel anxious, such as a friend texting her when she is too busy to text back; feeling she has too much on the go and not enough time; or getting in a fight with a friend and not knowing what to do about it.
- Making a plan before anxiety comes up, so she feels equipped for when she does become anxious. Ideas for this plan could include deep breathing, taking five minutes by herself to calm down, asking a friend for help, writing things down (either recording everything that is on her mind or just quickly making a to-do list on a sticky note).
- Teaching balanced thinking—positive thoughts to balance out negative thoughts. Draw a scale. In the middle write "Balanced"; on the right, write "Positive"; and on the left, "Negative." Ask her to write down some of her negative thoughts, such as *What did I do to make Keisha mad at me?* or *What if I don't have enough time to complete my homework?*

Then help her come up with opposite, positive thoughts to balance out her thinking—for instance, *I will talk to Keisha to find out how she is doing* and *I will do my best to complete my homework and I can ask for more time if I need it*. The goal is not unrealistically positive thinking, but balanced thinking.

- Creating an "anxious box" using a small box with a lid. Ask her to write out on pieces of paper what is making her feel anxious. The more specific the better: if she writes *Friends*, ask her to write down exactly what is happening with friends. Or she may volunteer, *I didn't understand the lesson from today*. Either put the box away for later, when she is ready to look at it, or add anxiety-management ideas for her to try. The purpose is to express anxiety—get it out of her head to where it becomes more clear, tangible... and manageable.

See Chapter 23's Connection Tool for tips for dealing with test anxiety

Gratitude 9

REMEMBER NAYA, from the previous chapter? As I was learning about Naya and the pattern of anxiety she was stuck in, she suddenly started going to school on Mondays. When I asked what accounted for the radical shift, the answer surprised me in its simplicity. Naya and her mom had decided on a routine whereby, at bedtime, Naya would count on the fingers of one hand what she was grateful for: her mom's freshly baked chocolate-chip cookies, nature walks with her dad, her cozy comforter, playing with her labradoodle, and eating M&M's. This easy ritual, practised nightly, did the trick. Soon Naya became what we called an "expert on her own anxiety," and she noticed when she started to feel "weird." She could sense her stomach tighten and her mind start to race as she began to worry about Monday. Because she was an expert on her own anxiety, Naya could use these signs to take action by talking to her mom—to get her anxiety out of her head, and to work on her action plan, which in this case was a perception shift. By focusing on what was good in her life, Naya became better at managing her anxiety about school, and she began to get good grades.

Many benefits come from even the simplest of gratitude practices. Dr. Lucie Hemmen says about gratitude, "You'll notice wonderful effects, including increased energy, improved relationships, improved mood, increased ability to forgive and feel empathy, and much more."[1] These effects can help when a girl's day goes sideways, when she can see only what's not working in her life, or when she gets caught in the cycle of complaining and venting. It can also help when she's feeling overwhelmed or stuck. Stepping away from a feeling, a thought, a situation, a relationship, an experience, or a problem in order to gain a different, wider perspective is important, and key to that new perspective, the bigger picture, is gratitude.

"Every time you are tempted to react in the same old way, ask if you want to be a prisoner of the past or a pioneer of the future." DEEPAK CHOPRA

I often use the metaphor of a camera with girls who feel stuck: when you zoom in, all you see are magnified details of the object; there is no room for anything else or any other interpretation. But when you zoom out, the object becomes smaller, less predominant, and there's room to see other objects.

It's all too easy for girls to focus on a single object, person, or idea, and to become consumed, even obsessed. It's easy to lose perspective amid drama. Girls can get caught in the web of chaos and have difficulty getting untangled. For example, girls are constantly trying to figure out who their BFFs are and who are frenemies, and this seems to change daily! Let's say that Lin learns that Isabel doesn't like her anymore. Likely, Lin feels rejected, sad, worried, and alone. Chances are she blames herself for the loss of Isabel's friendship and recounts what she may have done to cause it. Lin may also be thinking big thoughts, such as "I'll never have friends again!"

If Lin focuses on this one event, which feels devastating for her, her feelings will only become more exaggerated and take up a lot of mental space. It's time-consuming and exhausting! And it leaves little room for her to focus on other aspects of her life. Sometimes girls simply need to be reminded of their supportive family and friends. With a step back and a wider perspective on the situation, Lin will see that she does have kinder friends than Isabel, family members who love her, and many activities and events to look forward to. With a greater perspective, girls can come to see that there's so much more out there, and that they should not waste time having too narrow a focus.

But until she can generate this wider perspective, give her a hand surveying the options. One great way to restore a healthy perspective is to ask "Will this matter one day from now, one month from now, or one year from now?" And try to make her laugh. Laughter is a shortcut to lowering stress, changing perspectives, and activating the parasympathetic nervous system—the same response she gets when she knows she has a secure connection with you. Laughter truly is the best medicine, and science is beginning to prove it.[2]

When we encourage girls to focus on all they are grateful for, we help them generate positive emotions and radiate warmth to other aspects of their lives, even the little things—especially the little things. Gratitude for simple pleasures at home can carry over into gratitude for bigger blessings such as clean water and peace in our country. Sometimes this means asking her to look for things she typically takes for granted, such as a hot meal and a warm bed, or the details of her life that she may overlook, such as that she gets to go to school and be involved in after-school dance programs and weekend skiing adventures. Gratitude allows her to see all that is going well for her.

Gratitude helps her catch those moments of happiness as we taught her to do in Chapter 6. And a daily gratitude practice can even expand those feelings of happiness, so girls can really savour them; it will also help them be alert to catching more of those moments. Over time, the practice of gratitude becomes automatic and unconscious, and enables girls to pay attention, to appreciate, and to relish in *all* the moments that make up her day.

If there is one piece of advice you take from this book, make it this: a gratitude practice brings more immediate benefits than any sport, activity, or therapy ever will. And gratitude may be a great way to manage the anxious, avoidant behaviours so typical of girls when they feel worried about their tomorrow.

READ MORE

The Book of Awesome, by Neil Pasricha

Parenting a Teen Girl, by Dr. Lucie Hemmen

The Power of Now, by Eckhart Tolle

Taming Worry Dragons, by Jane E. Garland and Sandra L. Clark

CULTIVATING CONNECTION

Let's talk about:
- What gratitude is. Why is it important?
- What she is most grateful for.
- What "glass half full" means to her, and ways she can shift her focal point from what's not working and what she doesn't have to what is working and what she does have.
- How it is easy to have a narrow focus, and how much harder is to have a wider focus and the courage to be proactive and take action toward change.

Let's try:
- Taking five minutes at the end of each day for her to share what she is grateful for—it might be something as small as the candy she enjoyed or as big as earning a good grade on an assignment.
- Encouraging her to start a gratitude journal and spend time each day writing in it. You can keep one too, and/or schedule a daily or weekly time to check in and share. You may want to suggest starting with what she is grateful for in her day, and then ask her to consider her gratitude for what

she is learning at school (subjects, friendships, stress, and pressure), with her friends, and in her activities. She may want to add why she is grateful and give some explanation for her choices.

- Asking all the ways she can show gratitude in her life and what rituals she wants to set up (a simple thanks to people, thank-you notes, five minutes each day spent considering gratitude).

- Creating an ongoing gratitude list by taping several cue cards together, vertically. Ask her to write down or draw little things she is thankful for, using different coloured pens. This might be a friend smiling at her, a compliment from a teacher, or someone giving her a small gift. She can also cut out little pictures from magazines or use mementoes of moments she is thankful for—a candy wrapper, a movie ticket stub, a picture she took of a favourite moment. She can add as many cue cards as she wants, and this could be an ongoing practice that lasts for a while.

- Creating a list with two columns. Title the column on the left "What I Am Thankful for and What Is Going Well for Me." Title the column on the right "What I Am Wanting More of and What Could Be Better for Me." Have her add entries to each column. Then compare the two. Which has more ideas? Which has fewer ideas? Can she then create an action plan for how she can create even more of what she wants and address what could be better for her?

- Maintaining a healthy perspective by asking her: *Will this matter one day from now, one month from now, or one year from now?*

- Encouraging her to focus on herself and her own life more than on others and girl drama.

10 Exploring Spirituality

EVERY SO OFTEN, and to my great surprise and delight, the "big questions" find their way into my sessions with girls. Sometimes these questions are sparked by the lesson plans about different countries and peoples around the world, but sometimes they really seem to come out of nowhere. "What happens when we die—where do we go?" "Is heaven real and does everybody go there?" and "If Adam and Eve are real and God created the heavens and the Earth, why do we learn about the Big Bang theory at school?"

It is in these moments when I am faced with the challenge of how to navigate these questions around beliefs and spirituality that I feel most happy and proud, because these queries show me girls are wondering, and if they are wondering, they are thinking. I believe that one of the best ways for girls to understand themselves and their place in this world is to be curious about those questions that are beyond the scope of their daily experiences with school, friends, and family, and which contribute to a greater sense of meaning.

Spirituality means different things to different people, and I respect this. I believe that the most common threads between beliefs are the desire to consider what is beyond ourselves; the search for common purpose and meaning; the need for love; and the "golden rule" to treat others as we would want them to treat us.

A girl beginning to consider what spirituality means to her is an exciting moment. I don't feel I'm in a position to "teach" or impose my beliefs *onto* girls, but I am in a position to affirm their curiosity and encourage them to seek more knowledge and understanding. I understand its importance. In fact, a study at the University of British Columbia Okanagan found that children who are spiritual tend to be significantly happier individuals overall and have a deeper understanding of something greater than themselves.[1]

"Being on a spiritual path does not prevent you from facing times of darkness. But it teaches you how to use the darkness as a tool to grow." UNKNOWN

In an open and honest way, I explain that everyone holds their own ideas about spirituality. People may use different labels—God, a higher power, nature, the universe—and they may meet in different religious communities—at a mosque, a synagogue, a church, a temple, or a hall—but all beliefs are equally valid, and it is every girl's job to learn about spirituality so she can choose what it means to her. For girls, this learning might take the form of having conversations about core beliefs and values, asking close friends about what they believe in, and reading books that illustrate the variety of spiritual practices and explain the meaning and purpose of each.

As girls search for meaning in terms of their own spiritual development and growth, it's important for them to ask "What does spirituality mean to me?" and to understand that their answer to this fundamental question could influence every other aspect of their life. I know that when I feel spiritually grounded and safe and secure in spiritual traditions, I feel connected to

READ MORE

God in My Everything, by Ken Shigematsu

The Kids Book of World Religions, by Jennifer Glossop and John Mantha

others, to nature, and to the world around me. I also feel confident and strong.

Our pursuit of spirituality nourishes greater fulfillment and balance in life. As Ken Shigematsu, a close friend of mine, pastor, and author of the book *God in My Everything,* writes, "We crave depth, an experience of beauty, truth, and meaning." Girls are no exception—in my experience, their longing is as acute and honest as any adult's. It's imperative that girls explore spirituality and the interconnectedness between themselves, others, and another way of mattering in this world. Ken goes on to suggest that "we can learn to enjoy God's presence in our rhythms of work and rest, study and play, community and solitude."[2]

These "rhythms" could include daily prayers, affirmations, songs, sayings, or poems, and they can give us some structure to hold on to when life changes and feels uncertain. When girls recognize spirituality as an integral part of their daily lives, they can find a "rhythm" and meaning that works for them.

CULTIVATING CONNECTION

Let's talk about:

- Spirituality and what it means to you. Then ask her what it means to her.
- What you do when life throws you curveballs and becomes difficult.
- How she would explain the difference between spirituality and religion. (You may be surprised.) Listen to her guesses and musings about spirituality.
- What she feels are her core roots, and her values and beliefs about herself and the world.

- The ways in which honouring spirituality can make a difference in her life and overall health and happiness.

Let's try:
- Reading together. Books on kindness, justice, fairness, tolerance, and acceptance—all potentially spiritual topics.
- Seeking out spiritual leaders and mentors in the community who can speak with her and answer her questions.

PART TWO
A Girl's Journey Outward

Growing Strong
by Connecting in
Relationships

THE STRONGER AND more authentic a girl feels, the easier it is for her to embark on the journey of connecting outward in relationships with others. She can move from strength to strength, all the while taking time to care for herself, restore, rejuvenate, and think beyond herself.

If a girl feels insecure or uncertain about who she is, she can become an easy target for others to plant the seeds of self-doubt and self-criticism in her. Without a clear inward connection, a girl can easily become derailed by one dirty look, disparaging comment, or harsh criticism. When a girl feels good about herself, she will interact with others in a way similar to how she treats herself. Moreover, she will come to expect the respect and kindness she gives herself.

A strong girl is grounded in a sense of her own value; she is honest and open and can tell herself the truth about who she is, even in the face of social pressure. She will use her voice. She feels much more equipped and prepared to express herself, manage her own thinking, set firm boundaries, let go of unhealthy friendships, seek positive and healthy "tribe members," and create give-and-take relationships that are meaningful and fulfilling.

We can help a girl learn that when it comes to relationships, it is the quality of her connections that matters most, not the quantity—a lesson that just may conflict with the competing messages of social websites that promote the number of "friends," "likes," and "followers." A girl is hardwired to connect with the people in her life, so let's help her do so in positive ways by reminding her who she is, what she needs, and what she can learn by connecting in healthy relationships.

11   We Are Stronger Together

THE NUMBER ONE concern for girls—I know, because I've asked them—is friendships: making friends, keeping friends, and dealing with conflict with friends. When I hear their painful stories about backstabbing, changes in loyalty, and jealousies and competitiveness, I want to yell, "Can't we all just get along?" Unfortunately, relationships among girls are not that simple. If anything, they are actually very complex. Girls need to know: they are stronger together, and relationships must be nurtured in order to grow—something that comes as a girl learns to shift from feeling good about herself to feeling confident in her ability to extend herself and make connections with others.

Girls want to connect and build a community, a community in which they feel accepted, included, interconnected, secure enough to work through inevitable conflict, valued for exactly who they are, and free to express themselves. They want to feel warmth, care, support, and authentic and mutually trusting connections with other girls. The same impulse that drives her craving for security in connection with you motivates her to connect with her friends and to build her tribe.

Sometimes it is their intense focus on friendships that causes them so much stress and distress. They become confused and unclear about who their friends are, why they lose friends, and why friends can be so nice to them one day and so mean to them the next. And, in this confusion, she can often lose connection to herself—and there is nothing more dangerous for a girl than to fall into isolation and disconnection from herself.

What a girl often fails to see is that all girls have the same needs. This is the common humanity that Kristin Neff (see Chapter 3) points out as one of the central principles of self-compassion. Everyone needs to be seen, to be heard, to be accepted, and to feel like they matter. When girls can recognize themselves in others, they start to understand that they are all connected. It's unrealistic to expect that girls will become friends with *every other girl*, but we can expect that they will learn to respect and be kind to every other girl.

Focusing on what she shares with others will serve a girl as she develops all her relationships, from the tangential connections to the most significant, in her community building. Girls need to know how to be in relationships that are healthy, honest, authentic, and fulfilling.

Healthy Relationships

Healthy relationships for girls are ones founded on mutual respect, kindness, and care. There needs to be give and take, cooperation, and reciprocity, meaning that any one girl should not be the one doing all the work or compromising all the time. When she's the one putting in more than she is getting out of a friendship, the relationship is out of balance. This is unfair and unacceptable. Girls need to consider choosing other girls who support them, lift them up, and want the best for them (this means steering clear of girls who are too negative, critical, or jealous).

Healthy friendships also respect boundaries and differences. In healthy friendships, girls are able to have balanced conversations about wants and needs, and this in part means feeling comfortable speaking about anything. There is honesty and trust and real listening and understanding. Also, there should be fun and common interests. As girls connect more and feel a closer intimacy with their friends, they learn that they have support and loyalty, and that their closest friends will be there for them and stand up for them.

Girls can inspire and motivate their girlfriends to be their very best and to expand their possibilities. This is why we must remind girls to find friends who bring out the best in them and who push them toward reaching their goals. There's truth to the saying that we become just like the people with whom we surround ourselves.

Yet unhealthy relationships are all too common. Fortunately, most are relatively easy to spot. The "friend" looks like this: bossy, needy, disrespectful, and jealous. These girls may be abusive and mean on purpose, they may intend to be exclusive and leave other girls out, and they may really push and pressure girls beyond their comfort level. They never say "I'm sorry" or compromise, and they often embarrass their girlfriends in front of others and on purpose. Of course, it's important to build in some tease tolerance and resiliency to fun jokes and clowning around, so a girl needs to consider the difference between a joke and a mean comment in the guise of "just joking."

Positive Ways of Connecting

When girls are learning to connect and fit in, it can be easier to feel included by connecting in negative ways, but we need to show them the value of connecting in positive ways. For example, in order to gain approval and acceptance from a group, they may join in on gossip. After all, there's no quicker way to demonstrate that you're on the inside than to force another girl to the outside. But negative connections, as quick and easy as they are, do not last and can even backfire into loss of trust and superficiality. Ultimately, girls don't feel good when they fail in their attempts to form friendships or, in an attempt to gain social status, lose friends along the way.

Positive ways of connecting may take longer but are just as natural and easy to do. Girls can use relational tools such as compliments, sharing a little of who they are, looking more for points of connection than differences, asking questions, and initiating invitations. Girls can practise combining friendships with fitness, after-school activities, random acts of kindness, and community participation. With these positive tools, and a shift to activities they can do together, girls can maintain a sense of integrity and establish lasting, authentic, and meaningful connections with other girls.

When a girl struggles to connect in positive ways, a mentor's relationship with her can serve as a vital one, since it can provide an opportunity for both role modelling and teaching. Girls talking to their peers can be a great support, but mentors can matter more than peers. There may be nothing greater for a girl than being able to talk to someone who sees her potential (even before she does), who can point out her strengths and remind her of who she is and how she is changing. It is often through the eyes of another person that she comes to see what she can do and all she can be. Mentors, whether grandparents, teachers, or coaches, should strive to honour a girl's uniqueness, encourage her growth, strengthen her self-belief and self-confidence, and bring out her personal best. As well, girls may be more objective and less reactive with mentors than they are with an immediate family member, as the mentor is somewhat removed. Mentorships are intentional relationships that can help young girls grow even stronger and are a win-win situation for both participants.

Talking and Listening

I don't know if you've noticed, but girls love to talk. I asked one client what she had planned for the weekend, and she literally squealed with delight, exclaiming, "I love talking about me!" Young girls love to regale you with the highlights and lowlights of their day and share what's happening. Sometimes it's complaining and venting. Other times it's celebrating a success. So it's safe to say that girls like to talk, and I know you know how easy it is to get lost in the plot as they rattle off friends' names and who said what and why. However, girls benefit greatly from learning basic principles of communication: paying attention, staying positive, and finding balance.

We must ask our girls to apply the simple but underused skill of looking at the person they're speaking to. To really connect in conversation, we need eye contact and focused brains. And this means we need to limit distractions. Sometimes there are obvious distractions, like pens to fidget with or smartphones to peek at, but there are also less obvious distractions, like their own thinking, sleepiness, or disinterest. Encourage girls to put away distracting materials and make a conscious choice to be in the moment, paying attention. It shows respect for the person they are listening to, and models the kind of undivided attention they would like to receive when it's their turn to talk.

Girls can get caught up in gossip and complaints, and this is where we can use both empathy and what's known as the "redirect." We can remind girls that they can stay focused on positive aspects of people and use positive language with and about people without denying their own feelings or concerns. Sometimes girls just need to vent, and they need our empathy in order to feel heard and to feel that their feelings are being honoured. Expressing this empathy could be as simple as saying, "Wow, that sounds like a tough experience."

But other times, they need our help getting out of cycles of unproductive stories and thoughts that keep them stuck—they need us to show them how to let it go and make a change. Let's listen to girls' concerns and then ask for their buy-in on ideas and suggestions you may have. At the appropriate time, we can change the conversation (the "redirect") and help girls move out of rumi-nation by interrupting the going-nowhere cycle of complaining. This can be done with questions such as "What else is happening for you?" and "Can you tell me what you *like* about your friend-ship with Katie?" Again, this is not dismissive or uncaring, but there needs to be a limit to the *same old* conversation, which is neither healthy nor helpful.

Finally, we must teach girls that good communication is a bal-ance of listening and talking—perhaps not always, but usually. We can help girls practise the art of conversation: asking a ques-tion, *really* listening to the answer, and responding with genuine care. It is through sharing that a girl can come to understand the point of view of another and grow in her own worldview. If she talks over, interrupts, or talks without really listening, this will only frustrate other girls. The conversation can go back and forth like this: asking, sharing, and asking some more. Of course, the exception is when a friend is in need and requires her to listen more than share. Girls need to learn this too: sometimes the best help they can provide to a friend is just listening. Next time, it's them who can be listened to.

Popularity

Girls have a fascination with popularity. Popularity has its allure (not to mention the spike in dopamine, the pleasure chemical, that comes with elevated social status); girls equate being popular with being happy, feeling included, and a having a sense of belonging and self-worth. Many girls think that being popular is the same as being accepted or acceptable in the world. Striving for popularity is an impulse similar to wanting to feel "sexy" or famous. Once they have convinced themselves it is a healthy goal to strive for, girls strive considerably for it. What girls don't consider is popu-larity's dark underside.

Popularity is not good or bad, but it's often far more demanding than girls have considered, and the temptations to abandon positive ways of connecting and to slip out of life balance are many and often unforeseen. They find themselves in the spotlight they thought they wanted, but what they didn't foresee is what that spotlight experience is really like: they get watched more intently, imitated by many, evaluated and scrutinized, and gossiped about. There is also an inherent expectation that a popular girl will have an active online presence, updating her status daily or even multiple times a day, posting her best (sometimes provocative) selfies, and pretty much broadcasting her every move.

"I believe we can all come together, because if you take away the labels, you realize we're far more alike than we are different." ELLEN DEGENERES

When a girl is popular, she encounters new politics and new drama. The pressure to stay popular means being all the things that other people think that means. Sometimes this includes acting mean and domineering and abandoning the positive ways of connecting. It may include becoming strategic, aligning with the "right" people, and speaking the "right" language. It may include deciding whom to keep in her circle and whom to discard as her loyalties change, and the exhausting project of carefully thinking about social connections and invitations to events (whom to invite and whom to exclude).

Popularity is often a "no turning back" experience. Many girls who are considered popular have confided in me that, if given the choice, they wouldn't wish popularity on their worst enemy, and they'd let it go in a heartbeat in order to return to normalcy and be free to fly under the radar. Popularity, they say, is much too stressful and much too much work. Most girls, it seems, once having experienced the pitfalls of popularity, would trade anything to return to their old life.

BFFs

BFFs, or "best friends forever," has become a very popular term with girls, who are constantly searching for that one special person who will be in their life no matter what, forever and ever. They look for someone who is like them and who shares their interests and hobbies, someone who is loyal to them and will be there for them no matter what. This need for unconditional love and acceptance from a BFF while still a girl can later manifest in a desire for a romantic partner.

The problem I have with the term is that it's outrageously unrealistic and, I believe, an unhealthy approach to friendship. Girls are looking for a "perfect" friendship, but as we all know, perfection does not exist. Not only does the search for this perfection apply pressure on the girl searching—"Why don't I have a best friend?"—it also puts pressure on the selected friend to be all things, and exclusively committed, to one girl. Once a girl finds her BFF, she's often disappointed in her and hurt when her BFF wants to have other friends too. The very notion of two girls bound together exclusively can cause serious and unnecessary damage in girl groups.

Instead of a BFF, let's teach girls to consider having a circle of friends. Let's do away with a single "perfect" best friend, and help girls open up to a diversity of friends with a wide range of interests and personalities, and even ages. Girls need to consider being open and inclusive when it comes to the sisterhood or tribe they want to create.

A circle of friends should include people from many parts of her life—school, after-school activities, sports clubs, the neighbourhood, pets, and family friends. This circle should also include girls who are older than her, and younger girls too—age does not always match maturity or level of connection. Oftentimes, older girls are very positive role models and mentors, and younger girls may provide an opportunity for girls to mentor or teach.

We can also help girls look for friends who are like them and share similar interests and values, but also for friends who are not like them and may be interested in other activities. When girls are open to all types of people, those with different strengths and talents, they are more likely to learn from them. In this way, girls can be pushed out of their comfort zones and prompted to grow in positive ways.

A circle is flexible and accommodates fluidity in friendship. It allows each girl more space to follow her inner knowing, practise self-care, and adjust her life balance. It flows as friends come and go as the girls grow up and change. And a circle is great when there are friendship troubles (which is inevitable), because girls will know if one friendship isn't working, they have other options and many sources of support within their circle.

Let's teach girls to have circles of friends and to let go of the idea of having a BFF. Friendships are stronger, and girls can learn to be stronger inside healthy friendships, when girls choose variety, inclusivity, and flexibility.

Frenemies

"Frenemy": the creative, colloquial term merging "friend" with "enemy" to refer to a new type of relationship girls have that is neither always friendly nor always hostile; the other girl is sometimes a friend, then an enemy, and then back to being a friend. This is confusing! As adults, we have an easier time deciding either "Yes, I want to be friends with this person and keep them in my life" or "No, this person isn't working for me; I'll fade away." The term "frenemy" should not be equated with the term friendship.

Girls don't always know who is and isn't healthy for them, and it is much harder for them to "fade away," since most of their friends are girls they see every day at school. Often, letting go of one friendship that is not working means losing other friends in that same group—which, in a girl's mind, amounts to social suicide, as it may leave her feeling terribly alone and lonely.

The tricky thing about frenemies is that they act like they're great friends. Girls will love having a frenemy in her life: she can be a lot of fun, and she's interesting and exciting. Yet, *just like that,* the same amazing friend can be nasty and cruel and almost seem like a different person. Suddenly, she's the "devil," and this can be devastating for a girl. And then, *just like that,* the enemy will apologize and invite the girl to an event, say—and they are friends once again. From the outside, this looks like a damaging cycle of friendship abuse—friends one day, enemies the next. I doubt it could get any more baffling for a girl.

This is tough to watch and really tough to offer guidance on. Perhaps the best help we can give is to not comment on the frenemy herself (this will be interpreted as a personal attack) but discuss what healthy and unhealthy friendships are and let the girl decide. You can ask questions such as "How does a healthy friend make you feel?" This just may prompt the necessary self-reflection. Girls have a hard time breaking these cycles because the frenemy is often very present in her daily life; you can suggest ways to practise keeping a safe distance from behaviours she finds disturbing while she takes some time to figure things out and decide where she wants to place her boundaries. Also, sometimes the focus on the frenemy makes the girl loses perspective, and she is unable to "see" other people. You can guide her in widening her focus so as to pay attention to all her friends, and invite her to widen her friend circle. Reflection, distance, and variety can break the intensity of the cycle with a frenemy, and more often than not, when given these alternatives, girls can take the necessary steps to move away from their frenemies.

We cannot choose our girls' friends for them or tell them how unhealthy and inappropriate frenemies are. But we can open up the discussion and give them the space and tools to identify and choose healthier relationships. Strong and growing girls choose to be friends with girls who help them to grow in strength.

Working Through Conflict

Working through conflict can be one of the toughest challenges for a growing girl who is new to the world of social connections, both in person and online. She may not yet have the necessary coping tools to manage herself when things get tricky. For example, what is she to do when someone is mad at her, when she is on the receiving end of the "silent treatment," or when she says or does something she didn't mean to do, but the damage has been done? She most likely will want to avoid conflict altogether or feel tempted to be passive-aggressive and fight unfairly by telling every girl except the one involved how upset and angry she is. Girls have an indirect way of fighting that causes far more damage than if they were being direct, but somehow the indirect route is considered the safer choice.

We can decrease most of girl drama (more on that in Chapter 15) by urging girls to deal with conflict head-on: no passive-aggressiveness but sheer courage and boldness. We can teach girls to deal with conflict maturely and directly by creating easy-to-follow guiding principles: to always acknowledge when there is trouble, to talk only to the person involved, and to arrange a time to meet face to face that's good for both of them (never by text or posts).

Girls also need to know that it's unfair to gang up on one girl—that is, a group of girls against one girl—and that it's unfair to blame someone else solely for a problem (as any problem takes two). They also need to know that it's not fair to bring up the past (this is dirty fighting); rather, they should deal only with the present concern.

We can guide girls to speak with "I feel" statements, which are not accusing but, rather, allow them to express themselves, and to work together on finding a solution in which both girls feel heard and satisfied. And we can help girls speak directly and clearly. For instance, saying "I am concerned about how little time we are spending together lately" instead of "You seem really busy" or "I am feeling frustrated when we talk because I feel unheard" instead of "You talk too much." Girls, in their attempt to be "good," often use indirect, roundabout language. In an attempt to avoid hurt feelings, a girl will say something like "I am sort of not happy with the way you mocked me yesterday in front of everyone, and it would be kind of helpful if you didn't do that anymore. Is that okay?" But if we can help a girl working through conflict be direct and, at the same time, state what she wants and needs, it could sound like this: "I felt hurt when you mocked me. I need you to be more sensitive to my feelings when we are in group situations because I don't like this kind of attention."

It *is* possible for girls to work through conflict and disagreements, and when we help them through it, rather than around it, and guide them in fighting their own battles, we set them up for success in relationships as they grow.

CULTIVATING CONNECTION

Let's talk about:
- What a healthy friendship looks like: being friends with someone who treats her with respect and kindness, who is

READ MORE

Friends: Making Them & Keeping Them, by Patti Kelley Criswell

Odd Girl Out, by Rachel Simmons

Social Rules for Kids: The Top 100 Social Rules Kids Need to Succeed, by Susan Diamond

The Social Success Workbook for Teens, Barbara Cooper and Nancy Widdows

supportive and encouraging, and who pulls her up instead of pushing her down.

- What an unhealthy friendship looks like: being friends with someone who is mean or hurtful, who is jealous or rude, and who talks over her or doesn't let her have a turn.
- How to be open to new friends and connections, and why it's okay to let go of unhealthy friendships.
- Popularity: what it means to her to be popular—the pros and the cons, the pressures and the stressors.

Let's try:

- Showing her how to communicate positivity and friendliness: through eye contact, smiling, and open body language (how she stands, how she holds her head, where she places her hands).
- Practising active listening: focus on the speaker, show empathy, listen for feelings, validate what is said, paraphrase, and clarify the meaning.
- Seeking opportunities for her to be involved with other girls in the community and in activities she wants to do. Let her interests guide you.
- Brainstorming possible new and healthy connections for her and ways to meet other girls outside of school—for example, at soccer practice, at an art class, or in a community activity. Consider how to build a circle of friends, one that encompasses various ages, levels of maturity, and types of girls. The more diverse and inclusive the circle, the better.
- Teaching her to redirect conversation. Give her phrases to use that will help her from getting dragged into conversations about "who's prettier" or "who's smarter." She can say things like *I feel everyone is pretty and smart in different ways.*

- Role-playing to teach her to confront problems head-on. First, ask her what the situation is, and what she hopes to gain by confronting her concern. Decide on a scenario and create a script to prepare her to confront the concern. It could be asking the teacher for help, or telling a friend she changed her mind about an after-school activity. It may take a few "rewrites" to get the right words, but this process can help her feel empowered as she figures out what to say. Remind her to use assertive language such as *I feel I need to change our plans*—instead of *I am not really sure about today's plans.* Practising beforehand can help her feel more brave, courageous, and comfortable in the moment.

VIEW MORE

Mean Girls

Odd Girl Out

12   Words Matter

WORDS MATTER, OFTEN more than we think. If you look back on your own life, I'm sure you can remember the harsh words of a teacher or a judgmental comment by a close friend. Careless words often stick in our heads and can cause considerable hurt. How many times have we ourselves said something we later regretted saying? Perhaps we were stressed, we had a lot on our minds, or we simply got caught off-guard. Girls need to know that their words matter and that words cannot be taken back or "unposted." Despite our best intentions, words are powerful and can discourage and devastate. Yet words can often uplift and encourage too.

That is why we must be aware of and intentional with the words we choose when speaking to girls (and everyone else too, of course!). We must check ourselves before we speak. Simple questions to ask yourself are "What is my intention for saying what I want to say?" "How can I phrase what I need to say in a way that is both clear and kind?" "What would it be like to receive the words I'm about to convey?" And "Is there a way to watch my tone so as to sound caring and empathetic, not critical and judgmental?" I know, it sounds like a lot of work for a conversation. Think of it this way: time invested in the careful consideration of word choice can be time *saved* in potential miscommunication and misunderstanding.

We have all spoken in the heat of the moment, without thinking. Sometimes we think and speak simultaneously. We don't carefully consider every word we utter. But we do have time to think—for three critical seconds—before we speak or post.

"Watch your thoughts; they become words. Watch your words; they become actions. Watch your actions; they become habits. Watch your habits; they become character. Watch your character; it becomes your destiny." **LAO TZU**

Trisha Prabhu, in her inspirational TEDxTeen Talk "Rethink before You Type," passionately addresses the issue of cyberbullying among adolescents.[1] She introduces the non-invasive, non-intrusive, patent-pending computer software she created that incorporates a pop-up message that asks "Do you want to send this?" when it detects any inappropriate or potentially hurtful language. In her research, she found that when asked this candid question, 93 percent of adolescent posters chose *not* to send their intended, offensive message. This shows that a few seconds is all it takes for young people to stop themselves from saying things they don't mean or are best left unsaid.

This software is a reminder that we as adults also have the ability to stop and think before we speak to our girls: to think about our word choice and about our tone. "Did you do your homework yet?" can become "Please update me on your homework, and let me know if you need my help with anything." "Are you really going to wear *that*?" can be rephrased as "I'd love to know more about your choice of outfit today."

As you become more aware of your words and the power of your words with the girl in your life, an amazing thing happens.

As you change, she changes too. It's a ripple effect. Girls pick up and model not only what you say, but also how you say it. This means that if you are using kind and respectful language, she likely will too. If there is care and empathy behind your words, she will start to mirror your tone. And this means she can be encouraged to speak this way to herself and to her peers. She too can begin to realize her words matter, and that she needs to think before she speaks.

Girls can be confusing and unclear when they speak. How many times have you heard "I'm fine," only to find out later she's actually mad at you? How many times do girls say "I'm kidding" or "No offence but..." as a way of saying what they mean while avoiding repercussions? And how many times have you overheard girls talking about other girls in a negative and cruel way? Maybe you overhear her speaking with her friends when she's having a sleepover. Every ounce of you wants to interrupt her and teach her that her words might hurt, but you hold yourself back, knowing you'd completely embarrass her.

Again, this is why girls need us to model and then teach them that their words count too. Girls need to be fully accountable and responsible for their words—they should choose them carefully, and if they misspeak, they need to apologize. This includes online communication, which has made thoughtless communication all too easy. So a supplementary lesson on the power of words is this: whether spoken face to face or online from behind a screen of any kind, all words count.

Girls need to know that it's important to say what they mean and to mean what they say—and to make their voices heard. There is no reason to be deliberately convoluted or to sugar-coat a message, as long as she isn't being rude or inconsiderate of the other person's feelings. When girls focus on being clear, concise, and confident with their words, as well as caring and respectful, they can shape and influence others in impactful ways. When girls embrace the concept of "think before you speak (or type)," they can learn to be more sensitive to the effects of their words and to make good language choices. Words are powerful. Words matter.

VIEW MORE "Rethink before You Type," TEDx-Teen Talk by Trisha Prabhu

CULTIVATING CONNECTION

Let's talk about:

- How we might phrase what we want to say, knowing that the words we use matter. Choose curiosity over judgment. *I hear your idea, and my idea is different. Can I share my idea with you?* sounds so much better than *No way! You're wrong.*
- The power of words and how words have positive and negative associations. For example, the word "bossy" has a negative connotation (rude, abrasive, aggressive), but the word "leader" has a positive connotation (strong, independent, smart).
- How to be specific when asked "How are you?" Use details: *I am feeling very proud of myself today for all of my hard work on my science project* instead of vague statements like *Good* or *Fine.*
- Saying what she means and meaning what she says, and being thoughtful and confident with her words.

Let's try:

- Taking three seconds to think before you speak. In conversation with her, take turns taking the time to process the information and thinking about an appropriate response by counting on three fingers before saying anything.

- Prompting her to use the "gossip test." You might write these guidelines down as a gentle reminder that what she says about others matters. The gossip-test guidelines could include the questions *Is it true? Is it necessary?* and *Is it kind?*
- Choosing curiosity over judgment. For example, say *I am really curious about why you chose to cancel your plans with Emily to spend time with Suki* instead of *You cancelled on Emily again! How do you think that makes her feel?*
- Creating conversation cards she can use as options when practising to communicate clearly and with confidence when you ask "How are you?" but she doesn't know how she feels. On each card, write one option. Here are a few suggestions:
  > *I don't know how I am feeling.*
  > *I need more time to think about this question.*
  > *I am feeling many feelings and may need help sorting them all out.*
  > *I don't want to answer this question right now, but can you ask me again later?*
- Helping her practise apologizing authentically, for when she needs to take responsibility for her words. This might sound like *I am sorry for saying that you aren't a good friend. Next, time, I will be more mindful of what I say and how my words can hurt you.* Together, work on a rephrasing that sounds clear and concise while still conveying what she wishes to express.

Express Yourself   13

EVER WONDER HOW a girl goes from having "the best day ever" to having "the worst day ever"? It's shocking to see how quickly a girl's feelings can change; remember that girls too are often just as surprised by how overwhelming their emotions can be. And that is why, as girls' supporters and champions, we need to understand their emotions, validate their feelings, and help them explore and express themselves in healthy and constructive ways. Every girl must find her voice and be brave enough to express her feelings—and we can help her do that.

As girls' bodies change, their hormones often seem "out of control." Their hormonal fluctuations can account for increased sensitivity (especially to rejection), responsiveness to social stress, and their ability to be more acutely aware of subtle nuances in emotional tone. However, it's not correct or fair to attribute their roller-coaster moods to hormones entirely, as there is more to their growth and development. Having to deal with daily intricacies such as getting the silent treatment from a friend, deciding where to sit in the cafeteria at lunchtime, and updating her Facebook status is hard enough. But then there's managing friendships troubles, academic stressors, body changes and body image, and just plain figuring out who she is. These all contribute to mood fluctuations. And don't overlook the development of her brain—that plays a big part too. Her brain is sprouting, reorganizing, and pruning, and that influences how she feels, thinks, and acts.[1]

In her book *Untangled*, Dr. Lisa Damour says there are many factors besides hormones influencing a girl's moods, and that "the changes in [her] brain and the events that occur around her are more likely to shape her mood than the hormonal shifts occurring inside of her."[2] The brain starts to remodel itself during the early teenage years. The changes begin with the lower primal portions, then the upper outer areas. First, changes to the limbic system (the area of the brain relating to emotions and memories) heighten one's emotional reactions, and only later does the frontal cortex develop. Since the prefrontal cortex is the part of the brain where rational decisions are formed, this explains a lot about teens and their extra-sensitivity!

"It is a parent's responsibility to preserve the connection with their children, to preserve the relationship, so that the children can let go and become their own selves." DR. GORDON NEUFELD

As our girls grow and experience an array of different and sometimes confusing or erratic feelings, you have to know this: girls need to have their feelings heard, and the very best way you can support her is to validate her feelings and try to understand where she is coming from. Instead of dismissing feelings ("You shouldn't be that worried"), provide validation ("That is worrisome. Tell me more about your worry"). Rather than minimizing a feeling ("It's not that big of a deal"), honour the feeling ("You sound really disappointed"). When we validate their feelings, we teach girls to trust their feelings. And if she can trust her feelings, she can learn to trust herself. We need to keep in mind too that a girl's feelings are multi-layered, so the first feeling she shows is not necessarily her strongest feeling. Dig a little deeper. We often need to push her gently toward discovering what is below the trigger or surface feeling. Not accepting her first answer may look like judgment, but think of it as curiosity. Put your faith in her ability to stay with the process and get there on her own. This is how we grow strong girls who are equipped to investigate, accept, and express their feelings.

When talking to girls about their feelings, keep it simple. Feeling certain emotions—for instance, disappointment, worry, and fear—is often overwhelming for them, so help her keep things manageable and in check.

Emotions help a girl know what is happening on the inside, and they also give her information about what's going on around her. Feelings can be either "positive" or "negative"—both are good. Feelings come and go, and a healthy girl will become equipped to explore and accept hers, to breathe into and step into those feelings, and also to let go of those that are too overwhelming by expressing them. Emotions help her regulate and connect with herself, and give her life meaning.[3] Listening to music, singing, or playing a musical instrument can be a great entry point for exploring one's emotions and connecting with one's inner landscape. Music not only elicits emotions and memories, but can also help one identify and connect with a variety of feelings, from sadness and frustration to hope and excitement. Music can calm her, soothe her, and help her to release her emotions, lower her anxiety, and even boost her mood and energy level.

Girls need to know that their feelings are *their feelings* and as such are never wrong. Sometimes feelings can seem really big, as though they could swallow her up, and sometimes they can feel really small, and so be minimized or dismissed. Girls need to know that their feelings matter, and understand the importance of making self-expression a daily habit. When girls trust and confide in someone, they can experience that "me too" reciprocity of someone else sharing, and so truly understanding, their feelings.

Emotions Live in the Body: Notice, Name, Explore, and Express Them

When it comes to navigating feelings and putting them to good use, I have found this strategy useful: notice and name a feeling, explore it, and express it. Noticing and naming involves asking girls to observe their bodies and what is happening for them. It requires tuning in and resisting thoughts such as "I shouldn't feel this way." For example, a young girl might identify that she feels energy and a buzzing sensation quickly moving through her body, and she could then name this feeling "joy." There are many feelings, and girls need not limit themselves to being either "happy" or "sad." Providing a girl with emotional literacy allows her to be specific about how she is feeling. You'll find suggestions in the Connection Tool at the end of this chapter.

"The best and most beautiful things in the world cannot be seen or even touched. They must be felt with the heart." **HELEN KELLER**

Next, it helps for girls to explore why they feel the way they do. If we continue with the example of joy, you might ask, "What is joyful for you right now?" to which she may answer, "I just found out I did well on a language arts poetry project, and after school today, I'm meeting up with my best friend, Kayla."

Finally comes expression. There are definitely healthy ways of expressing emotions—laughing or crying, for instance—and unhealthy ways, such as throwing toys at her little brother or screaming at the top of her lungs. Sometimes, without being aware of it, girls externalize their unexpressed feelings. This means they put their feelings onto others (usually those they feel closest to, and yes, this means you!) so that they feel better and don't have to deal with the emotion. Other times girls internalize their emotions—bottling them up or blaming themselves. For example, she may have a fight with a friend, yet come home and appear happy. Inside, though, she feels that she is fully to blame for the conflict, even though in reality both girls contributed.

When a girl learns to express her feelings well and to put words to them, she is learning to tune in to herself—her true, whole self. She is also learning to feel connected to those closest to her. Expressing joy, for instance, may be a big smile, bright eyes, and a bouncing body, paired with the words "I feel overjoyed that I earned a place in the choir after rehearsing so much and believing I could do it." Help her to notice how it looks when she is exuding her joy. When girls express their feelings, they are also learning to experience them, especially difficult ones. We all know how much better it feels after we've unloaded in conversation with a friend after a long day.

Above all, remember that a girl's feelings are real, so always take them seriously. When feelings get tricky, girls can ignore, dismiss, deny, or suppress them. Although this strategy provides temporary relief, unexpressed feelings build up and will explode later on.

The More Difficult Emotions

Learning how to notice, name, explore, and express the positive emotions is what I call a day at the beach. You know—when you can enjoy every sight and sound, and life simply feels great. Dealing with negative emotions can be much more difficult. Brené Brown, in her TED Talk "The Power of Vulnerability," refers to it as the swamp.[4] Brown says we all have a natural tendency to want to avoid the swamp, and we do anything we can to avoid, deny, and run away from it, when what we need to do is find our way through. I agree—and it is of utmost important to help girls find the courage and the inner strength to wade through the swamp. My experience is that when girls do address their uncomfortable, negative feelings head-on, they not only feel relieved but also seem to discover a new-found sense of pride and confidence. What a valuable life tool!

Let's look at three of the more difficult or challenging emotions—anger, distress, and fear—and how we can help girls rely on their inner strength to work their way through them. A strong girl must learn how to make it through the swamp of these tough feelings, and we can wade in right next to her until she knows she can wade by herself.

Anger

Ask any girl when was the last time she got angry, or how she expressed her anger, and she'll likely stumble her way to a semblance of an answer: "Uh... um... I can't really remember when... I don't know..." Girls are neither clear nor confident when discussing anger because they do not feel entitled to be angry. In part, it's socialization ("good girls" don't get angry, remember?), and in part it's lack of confidence and a sense of self-worth.

Anger is a powerful and useful emotion. In short, anger lets girls know something is very wrong. It might be that someone has offended her or ignored a boundary she has set, or perhaps there has been a real injustice done to her or someone she knows. When we teach our girls to acknowledge their anger and then use it to take action, we are essentially teaching them to honour their inner strength and power.

Anger when turned inward can manifest as self-harm, self-hatred, or depression. Unexpressed anger can build up and become rage. Misdirected anger becomes projection. Anger, when avoided, becomes passive-aggressiveness. None of these management tools is effective because none is a direct expression of anger.

So what is most critical in order for anger to be put to good use is our teaching girls that anger can be a good thing. And discussing healthy ways to express anger: exercising, splatter painting, hitting a punching bag, yelling into a pillow. Discuss ways that will help her cool down, so that she can explore what exactly is triggering the angry response and then use language to express her anger to the appropriate person: "I am angry because..." followed by an action step such as "Here is a reminder of my boundary" or "I need to fight for this cause."

Distress and Fear

"Distress" refers to the feeling of pain, suffering, or anguish and usually stems from fear. When girls are in distress or fear mode, they tend to do one of two things: exaggerate their concerns *way* out of proportion, thereby catastrophizing the situation, or minimize their worry so that it's made to seem small and insignificant. Why? Because when girls are in an anxious state, their fear response and interpretations can be quick and extreme (thank you, amygdala!). They can overreact with the fight or flight response; this is the "hyperarousal state." Or they can freeze or underreact— the "hypoarousal state"—as a result of anxiety and emotions more than the actual facts or logic of the situation.

"The best way out is always through." ROBERT FROST

Their distress needs to be articulated so that it is brought into perspective. As they speak, they tend to soften, their emotions balancing out. To get girls to a place where they can provide themselves the balm of self-expression and manage feelings of distress, we have to really work at being there, listening and empathizing. This is where reflective language comes in handy. Phrases such as "Yes, I see," and "I hear your concerns," and "I understand why you feel this way" help girls find the safe landing space they need to get to a place of calm and centredness. When listening, refrain from offering advice or solutions. This is not what girls want or need in that moment. As they tell their stories and make sense of what's happening for them, they may be more open to our ideas, but tread carefully: always get buy-in first by asking questions like "I do have some ideas; are you interested in hearing them?"

Envy

Envy is a normal human emotion and a common one among girls. Girls know, first-hand, how difficult it is to watch another girl receive attention or experience success and not feel that she'd do anything to be *that girl*. Instead of feeling inspired and happy for someone else succeeding, girls may resent other girls and turn on them. I believe the most common reason for most bullying acts is envy. So what do we do to assist our girls in dealing with this feeling that could ultimately hold her back or have friends walk away from her?

First, use empathy skills—sometimes all it takes is acknowledgement that she is in a tough place. It's hard to feel envious and that we want what someone else has. Second, use envy as an entry point to discussing appreciation and inspiration. Envy could very be well be a sign that she is closer to knowing what she really wants. What is stopping her from setting new goals and feeling motivated to get busy on what she now sees in someone else? When girls can shift to self-development, they can feel confident and they can then be happy for others. Girls need to learn how to be happy for someone else's success and to celebrate with other girls.

It's important to start journeying alongside our girls in terms of their positive emotions, so that when it's time to explore negative emotions, they already have the tools and the practices they need to express themselves with self-compassion and strength.

CULTIVATING CONNECTION

Let's talk about:

- How feelings tell her how she is doing and what she may need to do.
- The important job of her noticing her feelings without judging herself.
- How feelings are fleeting. No one feeling will last forever, and the better she is able to accept her feelings with mindful awareness and without judgment, the easier it will be to move through them.
- The importance of always validating feelings; never dismissing or minimizing them. Use phrases such as *You sound happy* and *Tell me more about your frustration* instead of *You shouldn't be frustrated by that!*

Let's try:

- Spending a few minutes each day discussing feelings and what you notice about her. Ask: *What feelings did you experience today? What contributed to these feelings? I see you were smiling during your cross-country run; does this mean you felt you had a successful race? I see your eyes lowered; does this mean you feel disappointed?*
- Helping her build her emotion vocabulary with feeling words and the various reasons for her emotions. Ask her to explore why she feels what she feels. When you tell her how you feel, explain why. Exploring emotions takes practice and becomes easier as you put in the effort. (We could probably all use some practice.)
- Creating a "feelings thermometer." On a poster board, draw a thermometer on the left-hand side, as tall as the page.

READ MORE

The Feelings Book, by Dr. Lynda Madison

How to Talk So Kids Will Listen & Listen So Kids Will Talk, by Adele Faber and Elaine Mazlish

Untangled: Guiding Teenage Girls through the Seven Transitions into Adulthood, by Dr. Lisa Damour

Using different coloured pens, divide the thermometer into ten equal sections. Now list an emotion in each section, starting with the most negative at the bottom, and building up to the most positive. You might start with "Angry," for example, move to "Frustrated," then all the way up to "Elated" or "Excited." Beside each feeling word, write out a few ways of expressing that feeling. This poster can be added to as feelings arise. The more detailed the better. It's an effective way to understand the language of feelings, and also to start measuring and monitoring what the different feelings mean and look like.

- Creating a feelings booklet. Buy a basic notebook or journal with blank pages. At the top of the pages, write feeling words of your choosing, one per page. For example:

> *Happy*   > *Interesting*   > *Jealous*
> *Cheerful*   > *Relieved*   > *Lonely*
> *Sad*   > *Bored*   > *Confused*
> *Angry*   > *Silly*   > *Worried*

Below each feeling word, draw a big circle for the face, and add in the eyes, nose, and mouth that reflect that particular feeling word. At the bottom of each page, write why she might feel that emotion and how to express it in positive and healthy ways—for instance, taking a break, asking for help, writing in her journal, spending time colouring or drawing, or listening to music.

- Giving her a sample script for expressing her feelings, and practising together. For example:

I feel ——.

I feel this way because ——.

When I feel this way I can ——.

(Come up with ideas for healthy expressions of, and distractions from, feelings—going for a walk outside, playing with the dog, grabbing a hula hoop and twirling. Also come up with what you both agree are unhealthy distractions—posting a rant online or escaping into video games.)

CONNECTION TOOL
Feeling Words

To help a girl navigate her feelings, give her options. Have her choose a few feeling words each day to express how she is feeling inside. Remember, feelings are neither good nor bad; they simply *are*. Every feeling needs to be honoured.

• Happy	• Loved	• Disappointed
• Ecstatic	• Supported	• Frustrated
• Brave	• Surprised	• Left out
• Silly	• Kind	• Envious
• Joyful	• Shy	• Cranky
• Hopeful	• Sensitive	• Insecure
• Excited	• Disgusted	• Guilty
• Curious	• Mad	• Ashamed
• Proud	• Embarrassed	• Hurt
• Grateful	• Sorry	• Shocked

14   Navigating Change

CHANGE CAN BE difficult. Some girls look forward to change and embrace its newness, but most resist it and feel fearful and anxious about it. Some changes are predictable and some come without warning, but the one thing that's always true about change is that it is inevitable, so we must equip girls to accept and navigate it.

Certain changes for girls are expected and welcomed. Girls can love changing grades and moving up in school. They also look forward to getting older and being able to reach certain milestones of girlhood, like wearing makeup, spending time with friends without parental supervision, and, eventually, getting their driver's licence. I'm sure you've been privy to excited conversations about how they can't wait to be older—to be grown up—and have freedom and independence. Girls also love the changes they get to choose, including embracing new fashion styles, taking up different activities, and trying new sports.

However, life brings changes that take us by surprise—arriving without warning—and which give us no room for choice. These can knock girls off balance and contribute to feelings of being out of control and uncertain or insecure. Girls can resist growing up when they are not ready; they may not want their bodies to develop, and they may not want to have to face certain pressures, such as high school and new social circles, or romantic connections and dating. They haven't yet experienced many life changes, and they feel they will not know what to do. Girls can also get surprised by change—the sudden loss of a friend, a conversation that goes sideways, or a failing grade. This, as you know, can be painful to experience (for both of you).

Change can be uncomfortable, but resisting it is usually more so. In Part 1, I mention that Brené Brown refers to perfectionism as a way of trying to minimize or avoid pain. This behaviour is similar to trying to resist or avoid change. Knowing change is inevitable is a powerful piece of information.

"Any change, even a change for the better, is always accompanied by drawbacks and discomforts." ARNOLD BENNETT

Conversations about preparing for change can help. Talking about what "will be" and how they can manage newness helps girls reduce their worry about the unknown. Often the fear of the unknown is the real trigger, not the change itself.

We can help girls address fears and challenge each fear. For example, girls may worry that when they start at a new school, they won't have any friends there. Steer this discussion toward how to make friends, and use it as an opportunity to experiment with new tools, such as positive ways of connecting and initiating conversations. It's also useful to draw on past experiences, perhaps where girls have succeeded at making new friends, so that they realize they already have this skill.

Finally, to navigate change, a girl must manage the discomfort of not knowing, and this takes trust. When we assure girls that, although the unknown is uncomfortable, it will not always feel that way, they can begin to trust in the process. This is a tough sell, because no girl wants to be uncomfortable, but this is life,

READ MORE

The Girls' Guide to Growing Up: Choices and Changes in the Tween Years, by Terri Couwenhoven

and when girls practise working through the discomfort associated with change, they can come out the other side stronger and more trusting than ever before. We can also remind girls that discomfort is a sign they are changing and growing—something that should be celebrated!

CULTIVATING CONNECTION

Let's talk about:

- The many feelings that accompany change: excitement, enthusiasm, anticipation, fear, worry, and insecurity.
- Examples from her life. Which changes did she choose, and which changes "just happened"?
- Your own experience of change and what you do to navigate change in your own life.

Let's try:

- Writing about both the benefits and drawbacks of change.
- Breaking down change into smaller, more manageable pieces. For example, if a girl has to change her schedule, this can seem scary. To start, help her understand the reasons for the change and validate the feelings she may have about it. Then, take one step at a time: perhaps write her new schedule on the calendar and guide her in focusing on one day at a time. Always provide an opportunity for reflection at the end of the day.
- Changing on purpose. Switch up routines and patterns: change can bring new opportunities and a chance to meet new people and have new adventures.

Girls Can Be Mean 15

GIRLS CAN BE mean, and the sooner we accept that, the better. With eyes open to this possibility, we can actually support our girls, whether they are the mean girls or the mistreated ones.

Girl meanness manifests for several reasons. In a mean girl's attempt to establish her identity and fit in and feel connected, which includes her push for popularity and control, and her need for peer approval and group belonging, she begins to realize and assert her personal power and influence. Her desire for connection gone awry, she tests social boundaries, in the process showing jealousy and envy, and lack of empathy for others, as she tries to figure out what she can and cannot get away with. Sadly, mean girls are getting away with a lot these days, and many people are silently suffering. Mean girls seek connections at "all costs," meaning they'll do anything for power and the approval of those in the cliques that are forming; meanwhile, other girls, because of the same desire for connection, accept this abusive behaviour.

There is the obvious meanness that comes with overt bullying such as teasing, name calling, pushing, or pinching. And there is the covert bullying—gossiping, excluding, criticizing, telling secrets, whispering, telling inside jokes, betrayal, and turning on each other. These covert behaviours are usually hidden from adults and almost impossible to detect. Yet these forms of aggression are damaging to its targets.

The Hidden Needs
Behind Aggressiveness

Girls are exceptionally good at demonstrating aggressive behaviours, whether passive or covert. As Rachel Simmons explains in her book *Odd Girl Out: The Hidden Culture of Aggression in Girls*, girls are highly discouraged from engaging in open conflict or expressions of anger, which "forces their aggression into nonphysical, indirect, and covert forms. Girls use backbiting, exclusion, rumors, name-calling, and manipulation to inflict psychological pain on victimized targets... girls fight with body language and relationships instead of fists and knives. In this world, friendship is a weapon, and the sting of a shout pales in comparison to a day of someone's silence. There is no gesture more devastating than the back turning away."[1] Having worked with both bullies and girls getting bullied, I've seen this many times over.

"You can always tell who the strong women are. They're the ones building each other up instead of tearing each other down." UNKNOWN

This culture of aggression among girls, or girl meanness, is tricky to navigate for them because it's often "invisible" and almost impossible to gather evidence about or to prove. It definitely never helps when adults say trite things like "That's just girls being girls," as though this behaviour is a necessary rite of passage and a stage girls will grow out of.

Identifying aggressive behaviour—whether it is passive (as in aggression by inaction, for instance, sulking or deliberately being late because she is mad at a friend) or covert (aggression in the form of sneaky behaviour, such as a mean comment delivered with a smile)—can be difficult because accusing a girl of being aggressive can often worsen the behaviour and cause even more stress, worry, and isolation. When we start a conversation and connection with a girl who is acting in either a passively aggressive or covertly aggressive way, we need to come from a place of empathy, with the knowledge that behaviours happen for a reason. Why is she being passive-aggressive? Most likely the answer will take us to her inability to express herself. It's also very likely that she is hanging on to negative emotions such as anger and frustration. Her way of managing these feelings is to "get" others. Ultimately, it's a release and a sign that she needs more help working through her feelings and reconnecting with herself and her needs.

When it comes to supporting a girl who is having to deal with the aggressive behaviour of other girls, getting involved directly often fails. But what we can do is listen to her story; again, presence and being there for her are powerful (even though you may feel you are not doing enough). When girls know someone is there for them, and what is happening is not their fault, they feel a sense of relief. That is not to say girls are helpless in these circumstances. In fact, we can remind them that they can be strong and resilient by being aware of what is happening to them, and that they have what it takes to stand alone and align with teachers and allies at school. A girl can separate herself from passive-aggressive girls, remembering that what makes her strong is knowing who she is and what makes her unique. The hope is this: the "mean girls" around her will start to matter much less to her.

At its worst, girl meanness has very detrimental effects. Girls who are being mistreated may show physical symptoms—headaches, stomach aches, and muscle tension. They may refuse to go to school. If they make it to school, the anticipation of girl meanness may affect their ability to focus and learn, participate, and take on leadership roles. (An example: One client of mine seemed to be having great difficulty with math. Turns out, math was not the problem; rather, it was the terrible discomfort she was feeling in anticipation of the mean comments from the girls who sat beside her in the class.) A girl may begin to doubt herself and feel insecure, hesitate to take risks, and withdraw from her usual activities. She may begin to form a negative self-concept and experience feelings of loneliness, despair, sadness, depression, and disconnection. Sometimes these intense feelings can lead to self-harm and self-destructive choices.

We can challenge assumptions about girl meanness. Too often, people say things like "Girls will be girls" or "They'll grow out of it." It's true that girls are being girls and they may grow out of it, but at what cost? You may have heard precepts such as "It's a rite of passage" and "It's simply part of girlhood." Although it is fast becoming a seemingly socially acceptable norm, this does not mean it is in fact acceptable behaviour. We need to help girls on both ends of the girl-meanness spectrum, whether they are the aggressor or the victim. Girl meanness is not an acceptable way to gain power and social status, or for a girl to create her identity. Girls can have an active role and choice in how they treat others, and they can learn to take responsibility for the effects their actions have on others. A simple tool for a girl here is using empathy to imagine what it's like to walk a mile in another girl's shoes. Oftentimes, empathy can help her shift her connection to other girls from critical and mean to kind and connected. Consider, for example, if she were to find out that a so-called mean girl was being treated poorly at home by her family members; understanding her daily reality would help illuminate her unkind actions, even though it in no way justifies them.

Drama

Girl meanness and girl drama are BFFs, and they frequently have similar negative effects. Drama, or the unnecessary creation of something out of nothing, is typically based on misunderstanding and misinterpretation. It can also be the result of imaginary categories and the divisiveness girls use to criticize and put each other down. Drama can include spreading gossip and rumours, whispering and telling secrets, using indirect language and hinting, and uttering the ever-so-popular phrase "I'm mad at you, but I can't tell you why." Drama can be damaging, as it results in tears, fights, worry, confusion, loneliness, and the loss of friendships.

"Sometimes the easiest way to solve a problem is to stop participation in the problem." JONATHAN MEAD

The drama among girls makes some sense. It is, in essence, the result of disconnection, insecurity, and fear of social isolation. A growing girl is dealing with a lot: changing body and brain, fluctuating moods and emotions, trying to cope with everyday life without the necessary coping tools, and the developmental milestones of figuring out who she is and how she fits in. Add to the mix comparing and competing, jealousy and envy, changing friends and "frenemies," FOMO (fear of missing out), and insecurity and anxiety about feeling "not good enough" or as though she doesn't belong, and drama ensues. Girls may take on various roles, from starting the drama to moving the storyline along to simply enjoying the entertainment.

Girls—and you—need to know the drama is not a necessary part of girlhood, and girls do have the choice to stay away from the theatrics. A girl is free to walk away from drama, to decide she doesn't need to go along with girls who are starting it or stirring it up. To fit in socially, it may serve her well to listen to the drama and be the voice of reason and neutrality, perhaps even offering ideas and suggestions, but never exaggerating things. She can be the one who speaks directly, expressing her honest opinion. She can even shift the conversation by highlighting the positive qualities in the storyline or a person who is involved in the drama. By focusing on her own growth and what really matters, she can help or give back to others—and steer clear of or even eliminate the seemingly ubiquitous girl drama.

CULTIVATING CONNECTION

Let's talk about:
- What girl meanness looks like, and what it sounds like.
- The difference between overt and covert girl meanness and passive-aggressive meanness.
- Reasons for girl meanness.
- What it feels like to be mean, emotionally and physically.
- What it feels like when someone is mean to her.
- Reasons for drama and the damage that can result.
- How culture can influence the appeal and excitement of drama. What is she watching on TV or online that is overly dramatic (and influential)?
- Which role she tends to play in the drama. Is she starting the drama, passing on the drama, or absorbing it all and being entertained by the drama?

Let's try:
- Noticing girl meanness and pointing out a girl's social struggles and social behaviours. Say *This is what I notice about you* ... and ask *What do you notice?*
- Connecting with her by asking about friends and listening to her side of the story. Come from a place of empathy and understanding, and try not to "fix" or "solve" her problems. Helpful phrases to use are *That sounds tough* and *Relationships can be tricky.*

- Guiding her to articulate her concerns and problems, and encouraging her to begin by sticking to the facts. *Jackie is pulling other girls away from me at lunch time.* What does this mean? *I am alone at lunch.* What can she do? She can decide to eat lunch alone, she can find new classmates to eat lunch with, or she can ask Jackie to explain her behaviour. When emotions take over a girl's experience, it is very hard for her to see and sort through the truth of the matter.

- Encouraging her to use "trial and error" strategies to experiment with what to do in various social situations, as there is no single right answer. One time, she may try ignoring a friend who is being mean. Or she may try confronting her head-on by saying *That is mean and I am not okay with it.* Or she may try seeking out friends who are kind and caring toward her.

- Providing options for limiting drama, such as not adding to conversations that feel like gossip (in person, texting, and on social media), deciding not to hang out with girls who are overly dramatic, and blocking drama by changing the subject. Also consider teaching her phrases to use when faced with drama, for instance:
  I hear what you are saying about Amy, but I really like her because she is ——.
  Or
  I understand your problem with Jodi, and it sounds like you need to speak with her about it.

- Providing options for eliminating drama altogether: deciding not to watch reality-television shows that glorify drama, refraining from buying magazines, and deciding not to participate on certain social media sites.

READ MORE

The Drama Years: Real Girls Talk about Surviving Middle School, by Haley Kilpatrick with Whitney Joiner

A Smart Girl's Guide: Drama, Rumors & Secrets, by Nancy Holyoke

16   Set Your Boundaries

"YES" AND "NO": even these small words may be difficult for a girl to say when she wants to fit in and be liked so desperately; they are also powerful words when learning to set boundaries and establish limitations, even with you. Strong girls have strong boundaries, and they need to get comfortable using both words.

Some girls see boundaries as rules and restrictions, limiting their life experiences and keeping them from having fun. However, it's boundaries and guidelines that help to keep them safe and protected. Boundaries are necessary. Other girls have great difficulty setting boundaries because they are so used to putting others' needs first that they don't even think of their own needs, and because they often feel they don't have the right to. Let's teach them how to set boundaries and be confident in their self-worth.

At first, many girls learn boundaries at home; there are domestic boundaries around bedtime, mealtime, and homework time. Girls also learn boundaries at school: appropriate classroom behaviour, academic expectations, teacher expectations in the classroom, how to follow directions and complete assignments. As well, girls are learning social boundaries around relationships: how to behave socially and how to gain social acceptance, and how to manage problems that come their way.

I find, when I teach a girl about boundaries, that the best visual aid is a hula hoop. It provides a clear visual and allows her to see that she is at the centre of her own life. The hula hoop encircles her, as do her boundaries. She can then consider what she wants to allow inside her hula hoop (good friends, kindness, self-love) and what she wants to keep out of her hula hoop (mean girls, gossip, criticism). Hula hoops have proven to be a great learning tool when it comes to boundary awareness... and for having fun hula hooping afterward!

It is important that girls learn to set and keep boundaries as they navigate relationships. Conversations about boundaries can start with your asking, "What will you allow inside your hula hoop, and what do you want to keep outside?" Ask them to identify the qualities they are looking for in a friend, and the types of friends they want to have in their circle. Perhaps they want friends who are funny, kind, generous, outgoing, inclusive, athletic, or fun. Then ask them to consider what kinds of behaviours they will accept from others in their circle. For example, is it okay for a friend to joke about another girl in the circle or be sarcastic? What about gossiping about other girls? What about a friend who wants to exclude or bully other girls? Or a friend who simply pushes another out of her comfort zone?

These conversations need to happen so that girls consider what they want their boundaries to look like. We don't want girls to let everyone into their circle; conversely, we don't want girls to let nobody in. We can have these preventive and intentional conversations with them so they feel less confused and stressed out about relationships and more empowered to make good decisions on their own. With clear boundaries, she is also better able to ask for what she wants and needs from others: "I need you to listen to the story I want to share with you" or "I want to spend more time with you." When we prepare girls to be boundaried and discerning, their decisions about relationships become easier, and they stay safe and protected from toxic relationships; they also learn to decipher the difference between their feelings and the feelings of others. Sometimes a girl will "take on" another girl's feelings—but she needs to know someone else's feelings are not hers, and that she can have empathy and still be boundaried. She may let a friend's feelings inside her hula hoop, but she is more aware of her decision to do so.

Setting boundaries is the easy part; keeping those boundaries can prove more difficult. We need to teach girls to be aware of "boundary pushers"—people who will try to step inside her hula hoop. This can be tricky, especially when sometimes we are the boundary pushers, and because many girls are so used to giving in. This may sound familiar: she may say she doesn't want to talk to us, but we keep asking questions. Believe me, I've done this many times myself! We must listen and respect what she's telling us, then allow her to talk to us when she is ready. We cannot expect her to be ready to talk to us just because we're ready. As you've probably noticed, without her consent or buy-in, you won't get anywhere.

There are girls who understand no means no and hold their boundaries firm; many girls, however, ignore their boundaries and feel that no means maybe. They are often uncomfortable and want to maintain their "good girl" image. They fall into patterns of people pleasing and conflict avoidance. But if we remind girls over and over again that they need to always be safe inside their hula hoop and feel safe in relationships, they will learn to push back. "Push back" is when girls firmly remind others of their needs and decisions. It may sound like this: "Again, I don't want to go to the park after school" or "I've decided that I don't want to talk about Paige—let's talk about something else."

If they can't seem to come up with this push-back language on their own, lend them options so they can practise assertiveness. And being firm with their boundaries may take some practice. What they say needs to be clear, simple, and repeated if necessary. It requires a confident stance, no smiling, clear and firm language, and a voice that is audible. Then girls need to learn to walk away and not worry or think about what the other person is going to say or do.

When girls set and keep boundaries, especially with social media, maintaining privacy, they become stronger and build protections around that strength so that they can develop even further. Let me assure you, it feels great to see girls who understand that they don't have to compromise to meet the needs of others or accept behaviours that do not align with their values. Boundary pushers who are accustomed to disrespecting the sanctity of the hula hoop, beware: once girls let go of the "good girl" image, they become strong and boundaried girls.

CULTIVATING CONNECTION

Let's talk about:
- Boundaries and how they keep girls safe and healthy.
- Her right to have personal boundaries and how to take responsibility for how she allows others to treat her.
- Recognizing that other people's feelings and needs are not more important than hers.
- What she wants to invite into her hula hoop, and what she wants to keep out of her hula hoop.

Let's try:
- Drawing a hula hoop on a piece of paper and having her identify which friends she will allow inside her hula hoop and which she wants to keep out. Repeat the exercise with other things besides names of friends—consider qualities in friends; kinds of language; and examples of gossip, sarcasm, meanness, silliness, fun, and peer pressure. Using a

READ MORE

*Boundaries:
When to Say
Yes, How to
Say No, to
Take Control
of Our Life*, by
Henry Cloud

*A Young
Woman's
Guide to
Setting
Boundaries*,
by Allison
Bottke

real hula hoop, write these qualities and examples on cue cards, placing the cards around her on the floor, either inside or outside her hula hoop as appropriate. It will be very helpful for her to have something tangible to hold on to and a visual reminder once she continues with her day.

- Saying no. Think of a series of requests (from simple to more difficult), and have her practise saying no with confidence and by using a simple phrase. You could start with "Can I use your iPhone?" or "Would you like pizza for dinner?" and then try more challenging questions that may conflict with her values, such as "Do you want to go to the park with me, but not invite Kendall?" or "Should we post that silly picture of Arianna so she feels embarrassed?" Ask her how it feels to say no and what feelings come up for her during the entire exercise. Remind her that setting boundaries takes practice and will get easier.

CONNECTION TOOL
Qualities Worth Cultivating

In supporting a girl in knowing who she is, explore what she values the most in herself. If she has difficulty, start by choosing the qualities you see in her (see the list below for ideas). Then, ask her for an example of how she shows each quality. For instance, if she chooses "adventurousness" as one of her core values, ask her how she shows she is adventurous. She may say, "I am adventurous when I try a new activity without fear or hesitation and give it my all."

To extend this activity, ask her to choose a quality each week, with the intention of seeking various ways to exemplify the quality. Talk about empowerment!

- Adventurousness
- Ambition
- Assertiveness
- Artistry
- Attractiveness
- Boldness
- Care
- Charm
- Cheerfulness
- Clarity
- Cleanliness
- Compassion
- Confidence
- Courage
- Creativity
- Daringness
- Dependability
- Empathy

- Energy
- Expressiveness
- Extroversion
- Faithfulness
- Fitness
- Flexibility
- Friendliness
- Happiness
- Health
- Helpfulness
- Honesty
- Humility
- Humour
- Independence
- Intelligence
- Introversion
- Inventiveness
- Kindness

- Logic
- Love
- Loyalty
- Optimism
- Patience
- Perceptiveness
- Pleasure
- Resourcefulness
- Reverence
- Security
- Self-Awareness
- Simplicity
- Straightforward-ness
- Strength
- Trustworthiness
- Wealth
- Wisdom

Confident,

17 Not Conceited

NOT EVERYONE CAN take a compliment. Receiving kind words from others is something that can be difficult. Girls, especially, can ignore, dismiss, or minimize compliments, or even talk away a compliment. This is what it sounds like:

Kiera: *Harjeet, I love your shirt. You look so pretty today.*
Harjeet: *This old thing? I've had it forever.*

Girls seem to really struggle in accepting words that are intended to encourage, support, and validate. So why, with words intended to make them feel good, do girls put up their shields to deflect any goodness?

Even if, deep down, they really *want* to believe the compliment and feel good about themselves, girls tend to discount compliments because of how they've been socialized. They worry that agreeing with a compliment will be interpreted as their being conceited. They fear being judged and rejected and will almost always make what they consider to be the safer choice: self-deprecation, staying unnoticed, flying under the radar. Let's delve into this a bit more.

First of all, girls often confuse confidence with conceit. Self-confidence may feel like conceit, but it is not the same thing. Self-confidence is when girls believe in themselves and their strengths, abilities, and talents. And when they can recognize the hard work they put forth and the results that emerge, and that they have earned the right to be proud of their achievements and accomplishments. Being conceited, on the other hand, involves comparing themselves to other girls so that they may feel elevated and better than their peers. Conceit actually creates a false confidence and can make others feel badly too. It can also damage social connections—who wants to be friends with a boaster?

"I get worried for young girls sometimes: I want them to feel that they can be sassy and full and weird and geeky and smart and independent. And not so withered and shrivelled." AMY POEHLER

Confidence sounds like this: "I feel great in my new outfit! I'm so happy with my purchase!" Whereas conceit sounds like this: "My outfit is way better than what *she* is wearing, and I look better than anyone else!" This kind of comparative language is not a healthy quality and may be a sign of perfectionism. Confident language, which doesn't involve comparisons, comes from a place of security and authenticity, knowing that we can be "perfectly imperfect," whereas conceited language comes from a place of insecurity and competition, and reeks of the need to be noticed.

The second reason it can be so difficult for girls to accept compliments is that they see doing so as dangerous. They might not admit this, but accepting positive feedback can, ironically, make them feel as if they are awfully close to criticism. In a sense, accepting a compliment is a risk because it's a way of demonstrating that we are hearing and taking in what others want to reflect to us: today it may be a compliment I'm being offered, but what if tomorrow it's a criticism?

We can show girls that accepting the observations and feedback of others (both positive and negative) is a way to grow.

Confidence comes from knowing what they are good at, but also from not denying that there are things they could improve upon. Confidence requires awareness of and honesty about how they are imperfect, and being "perfectly imperfect" means being vulnerable.

Girls may see exuding confidence as something that attracts judgment or exclusion; unfortunately, sometimes it does. However, we can help girls stand in their strength and embrace confidence. Step one is to show them how to graciously accept compliments. This one is easy. I can tell you how it's done. With only two simple words: "Thank you."

CULTIVATING CONNECTION

Let's talk about:

- Ways she can show her confidence. What are her strengths, and how does she show these strengths?
- What "conceited" means, and what conceited statements sound like. Ask her if she thinks she is conceited and why.

Let's try:

- Teaching her to accept compliments graciously (instead of dismissing them) and to say a simple "Thank you" with a smile, knowing that taking a compliment does not mean that she is bragging or boasting.
- Teaching her to give compliments to others and even helping other girls accept their compliments.
- Helping her practise assertiveness: ordering at a restaurant, paying for her clothing at the mall, answering the phone, buying a movie ticket.
- Teaching her to assert herself and express her opinion,

perhaps even starting with *I agree* or *I disagree* and then adding reasons for her opinion. Teach her to not go quiet or fade away when others hold a different opinion from her.

- Talking to her about how to deal with peers who are using self-deprecating language or who are overly competitive—girls do not have to model this language, and they do not have to accept it. A phrase such as *We all have different strengths and areas of growth; what are yours?* could be something she says when she encounters a peer who doesn't seem to have confidence when she speaks.

- Practising strong and confident language. Instead of expressing worry, use strong and powerful phrases such as *I can do anything I want* and *This looks tough, but I know I will try my best*. For more positive power statements, see Resource 2.

- Practising strong and confident body language: standing tall, shoulders back, eye contact, and head held high. For more about strong body language, see Resource 7.

- Creating a self-worth manifesto, or reciting the one provided in Resource 1.

18 Social Media and Keeping It Real

GIRLS ARE SPENDING more and more time "connecting" on social media and less and less time connecting in person. Did you know that the average seven-year-old will have already watched screen media for more than one full year of twenty-four-hour days?[1] It's also next to impossible to hold their attention; they want to check their devices every few minutes, and text, tweet, post, message, or snap. This sure feels frustrating when you yourself simply want a real connection with her.

Remember, it's the job of adults to show our girls what real connection looks and feels like. Social media provides a sense of belonging, but one that is impoverished compared with the real thing. It masquerades as a way to connect everyone, yet, more than ever before, girls are reporting feeling less connected, more isolated, and more alone. Having virtual "friends" may never feel as good as does the warmth and rewards that in-person friendships offer. Social media enables girls to avoid problems instead of facing them head-on. It is in part responsible for the decline in social and communication skills. Instead of real relationships, she may just be creating digital drama and expanding her digital footprint.

A girl who is savvy on social media may not be paying attention to the fact that what she shares says a lot about her and may have long-lasting detrimental effects on her reputation. Girls like to call their posts "artsy"—translation: "not appropriate"—which may include photos taken in the bedroom or showing way too much skin.

Essentially, the potential downside of social media can be summed up in two words: distraction and damage.

"Social media has given us this idea that we should all have a posse of friends, when in reality, if we have one or two really good friends, we are lucky." BRENÉ BROWN

Social media does also have its benefits: it enables her to stay in touch with faraway family and friends, to get help instantly (as well as immediate information and news), to feel "normal" by reading other girls' posts and chatting in familiar chat rooms, and to have fun and excitement as her network develops and she learns new things about the people she knows. You may be surprised by just how thoughtful and intentional a strong girl will be online when she feels secure and confident—writing comments of genuine praise, being curious, and developing and sharing her opinion in conversation with people in her network.

However, despite the many advantages social media holds, it has many more pitfalls, including cyberbullying, superficial connections, and what I call "post and run." Girls are hiding behind their screens, saying whatever they want and not feeling accountable for their words. But as those on the receiving end know well, words matter. It would be nice if everyone took a three-second pause before they hit Post.

Social media ignites much damage, as girls who are typically sensitive, empathetic, and logical are now posting anything they want, without consideration of how their post may affect others.

READ MORE

*American Girls:
Social Media
and the Secret
Lives of Teenag-
ers,* by Nancy
Jo Sales

*It's Compli-
cated: The
Social Lives
of Networked
Teens,* by
Danah Boyd

Girls are also failing to consider that their online presence, through inappropriate posts and unfiltered messages, may damage their reputations, affecting future academic scholarships, applications to post-secondary institutions, and even employment opportunities. Girls need to know that nothing online is truly private, and that once something is online, it cannot be taken back.

Lastly, cyberbullying is all too easy. It is easy for predators and bullies to harass girls who are overfriending and oversharing online. Cyberbullying is a silent pandemic that can leave girls feeling traumatized and ashamed. Cyberbullies are the online equivalent of the boundary pushers we met in Chapter 16. If you have concerns about how much a girl is sharing online, it wouldn't hurt to pull out the hula hoop.

Girls need to be aware of their safety online, and they must feel they can come to you with any of their social media distractions or damages. Girls are hardwired to connect with the people in their lives, so let's help them come to us first, and let's work hard to model for them what healthy relationships and boundaries feel like, in person and online. And yes, this might even mean she finally accepts your friend request!

CULTIVATING CONNECTION

Let's talk about:
- What is and what is not appropriate to share online—for instance, posting a funny joke or details about an important event, but not posting the details of your family's upcoming vacation; posting photos she took with a friend to post on Facebook, but not posting photos of friends without their permission.

- Which of her friends she feels overfriends and overshares, and the reasons they may be making those choices.
- Your expectations of social media and online safety guidelines. Help her to consider her online presence. She may not consider how what she puts out there in the virtual world may affect her later in life. Let her know that if she gets into trouble online, she can come to you—no matter what.
- The pros and cons of sending a text message or posting online. For example, sending a message can be fun and exciting; not sending it means you won't have to worry about who sees it or comments on it.

VIEW MORE

"Rethink before You Type," TEDx-Teen Talk by Trisha Prabhu

"Quit Social Media," TEDx Talk by Dr. Cal Newport

Let's try:
- Asking her to check in with herself about how she feels after spending time on social media. Guide her to gauge her own experience: Does she feel tired or trance-like? Does anything she views disturb or confuse her? Does she feel happy and inspired by her time spent online?
- Providing her with strategies to deal with mean or hurtful posts and messages, such as immediately deleting them or just not even responding, and with predetermined responses she can say aloud or type in response, such as *That's not for me! I'd prefer not to. We're going to have to agree to disagree.* And don't forget about the always useful *I need more time to think about this*, as you learned in Chapter 12. You may want to post these messages on sticky notes somewhere visible so she sees them and can put them into practice when these tricky situations come up.
- Establishing rules and guidelines on media use and screen time: times of use, duration of use, number of times per day,

where it's permissible (open, common areas are best), and keeping passwords private. Decide, together, which sites are healthy and appropriate. Be clear that if guidelines are broken, there will be consequences, such as loss of privileges.

- Competing with technology: plan activities and outings to encourage off-screen time. Plan outdoor events and other in-person activities that she can get excited about. Unplug to connect!
- Having real conversations, with eye contact and no technological devices. Have consistent and ongoing conversations in real life about what's going on in her online world. Have these conversations before there is conflict.

Screen Time and
the Tangled Web   19

GIRLS ARE NAVIGATING a new landscape because screens and technology are intertwined with culture, economics, politics, education, and their environment. We all use screens daily, for information, entertainment, social connection, and even emotional self-regulation. That last one may sound a bit complicated, but all it refers to is calming yourself down when you feel anxious or psyching yourself up if you feel depressed, for example, when you arrive a few minutes early to an event, feeling a bit awkward, and immediately grab your phone and look down at the screen. In a moment of discomfort, anxiety, or boredom, a girl will grab her phone and look at her texts, tweets, snaps, and updates, maybe clear out all the notifications and refresh each app—sometimes more than once—until something else demands her attention.

As the role of technology becomes greater in a girl's life, and the possibility of screen addiction—reliance on a screen for fulfillment—is a growing concern, we need to consider small ways to intervene and help her untangle this complicated web of technology and false connection. A girl can easily be getting screen time from waking to bedtime. A shocking 39 percent actually even sleep with their cell phones.[1] The average girl spends between three and a half hours and six hours per day looking at a screen.[2] The blue spectrum light emitted by screens can disrupt the body's melatonin (the sleep hormone) and make the brain think it's not tired—which may explain why she feels wide awake even though it's time for bed.

Screen time makes sense, but the accompanying anxiety can be detrimental to a growing girl's coping skills. The more anxious she feels, the more screen time she will want. This way of self-regulating is not healthy, but it works. She'll grab her phone to escape an anxious moment, and she will feel relieved and maybe even calm. But in the long term, she needs to learn how to notice and manage her own anxiety. If she can implement the management tools from Chapter 8 instead of turning to technology for a quick escape and a reprieve from discomfort, she will become more aware of and attuned to what is happening in her body, connect to her sensory experience, calm herself down with deep breathing, and check in and then reframe her thoughts, shifting from the "What if?" worry thoughts to the focus on what is happening and what is true.

"The earlier we introduce screens, the more it affects the child's brain development and the more likely they will have trouble managing their addiction to screens and technology later in life." DR. LAURA MARKHAM

Technology time can take away from her time spent in live connections, hands-on activities, and lived experiences, including moments of uncertainty and confusion. Technology can serve as an escape when stressed, a calming tool when anxious, a "friend" when faced with loneliness, and a "mentor" when she needs advice or guidance. We have learned a lot about the necessity of hands-on experiences and how the brain learns from the sensory experience by studying sensory play. We know that "young children are oriented toward sensory experiences. From birth, children have learned about the world by touching, tasting, smelling, seeing, and hearing. Sensory play also contributes in crucial ways to brain development. Think of it as 'food for the brain.' Stimulating the senses sends signals to children's brains that help to strengthen neural pathways important for all types of learning."[3]

As girls become increasingly dependent on technology for connecting, feeling as though they belong, and destressing themselves, they are losing the opportunities to connect in real, meaningful ways; to learn coping skills and healthy self-regulation for managing their emotions; time for self-reflection; and the ability to be in the moment, noticing and appreciating what is around them. As technology journalist Nicholas G. Carr observes in his book *The Shallows: What the Internet Is Doing to Our Brains*, "Just as neurons that fire together wire together, neurons that don't fire together don't wire together. As the time we spend scanning Web pages crowds out the time we spend reading books, as the time we spend exchanging bite-sized text messages crowds out the time we spend composing sentences and paragraphs, as the time we spend hopping across links crowds out the time we devote to quiet contemplation, the circuits that support those old intellectual functions and pursuits weaken and begin to break apart."[4]

Technology is taking over, and the balance of virtual life to "real" life is one we need to help girls recalibrate. How do we do it? To start, help her make sense of the information she's consuming. Sometimes she'll get overwhelmed and even scared, especially if she is tempted by "clickbait," content on the Internet (often sensational or provocative) whose main purpose is to attract attention and draw visitors to a particular webpage. Lead her through conversations, as you did about how some media profits from making people feel bad about themselves, so she learns to develop a healthy skepticism about articles she reads online. As technology changes and advances, continue to educate her on the influence of dependence on screens, and challenge her to find alternatives to screen time, technology escape, and using screens as a tool for coping. Help her to explore a new landscape, one with a balance of virtual and real-life living.

READ MORE

Digital Kids: How to Balance Screen Time, and Why It Matters, by Martin L. Kutscher and Natalie Rosin

Reset Your Child's Brain: A Four-Week Plan to End Meltdowns, Raise Grades, and Boost Social Skills by Reversing the Effects of Electronic Screen-Time, by Victoria L. Dunckley

CULTIVATING CONNECTION

Let's talk about:

- The necessity of real, hands-on experiences and how the brain learns from the sensory experience.
- Real relationships with peers, friends, family, and mentors— people she can talk to about her thoughts and feelings and what's really going on for her.
- The risks related to technology, including addiction, substituting virtual friendship for in-person friendship, and clicking on links to sites that are unhealthy and unsafe.
- A cut-off time for screens in the evenings, and all Web-enabled devices staying out of the bedroom.
- The need to be more aware of what she is viewing, and that you are available for support should she get into trouble online.
- Self-regulation and alternative ways to calm herself down and manage her emotions—deep breathing, sitting in silence, or exploring and expressing her feelings.
- Internet safety, especially tempting clickbait that takes the viewer to advertising, risqué images, fake news, or inappropriate content.

Let's try:

- Experimenting with her maximum threshold for technology. Sit beside her as she begins to view Web content on a screen in her normal fashion. Start a timer that counts up (or make a note of the time), and every few minutes ask her to notice her body, especially her eyes and head. As soon as she gets the "screen zone" feeling (you can let her define this—it won't feel good), stop the timer (or note the time). The number of minutes that have passed is her threshold, or the maximum she should be on a screen before taking a break.

- Reading books in print, instead of onscreen, for higher-quality sensory learning.

- Making more time for talking about feelings. Explore with her how she is feeling, what she is experiencing, how she is coping, and creative ideas for coping in the future.

- Finding alternatives to technology as a source of connection: try partnering her with a mentor, signing her up for community classes, or suggesting she volunteer for an organization or learn a new skill.

- Teaching her how to be bored. Boredom isn't a bad thing. In fact, it can serve as a time to reflect and notice. Oftentimes, it is through boredom, stillness, and daydreaming that she will come up with her best, most creative ideas. Boredom is a necessary part of creativity and growing.

- Being involved in her online world. Be available should she have any questions or concerns, especially when things go badly for her.

TRY THESE APPS

f.lux

Rain Rain Sleep Sounds

Relax Melodies: Sleep Sounds, White Noise & Fan

PART THREE
A Girl's Journey Onward

Growing Strong by Connecting in School, Work, and Life

WHEN A GIRL feels a strong connection to herself and in the relationships she forms with others, she grows in her ability to extend herself into even deeper and more meaningful connections. She begins to consider the interconnectedness between herself and the world.

At first, a girl's connection to the world is school—this is where she has the opportunity to think about who she is in a global context. From a simple beginning—asking "What do I know?" and "What kind of student am I?"—her self-concept and worldview can become shaped by everything she learns about other peoples, cultures, and customs, and she comes to understand how vast the world is and that she has a unique place and purpose in it. The questions then evolve into "What is my purpose?" and "What difference do I want to make?"

A strong girl wonders what she can do to help people beyond herself and her family—people in her neighbourhood and in society. She expands her thinking beyond name brands and popularity to include wonder, wisdom, and generosity. She feels the needs we all share: for love, acceptance, belonging, and purpose. When she learns about the power of setting goals, self-motivation, taking positive risks, and working hard, she will realize that with determination, effort, and passion, she can do anything.

We can help her cultivate her connection to her world by encouraging her to reflect upon her sense of belonging as well as on her understanding of difference and sameness with others. We can begin the conversations about passion and purpose, praise her efforts as equally as her achievements, and remind her that she can make a difference—she simply needs to decide *how* and then work hard toward what she really wants. When focused on the bigger picture, she is much less likely to get distracted by the daily concerns in her life, because she will be thinking about her connection with the world and her higher purpose.

Turning Setbacks

20 into Comebacks

"TURN SETBACKS INTO COMEBACKS." I read this phrase on Instagram and loved it! So often, girls feel down and out about mistakes or failure in their lives. When girls experience setbacks, they can feel as if all their energy has drained from them and they have nothing left to offer.

Failure, for girls, could be failing a test or failing to be organized and forgetting to hand in assignments. It could be not doing well at a swim meet or in a dance competition. Failure can mean not getting invited to a party or fighting with a friend. For a perfectionist, failure is anything less than perfect and polished, anything less than complete success (see Chapter 3 for more on perfectionism). But girls need to know that failure is a fact ("I failed"), not a character flaw ("I am a failure"). There's a big difference.

News flash: Failure is good! When I was in grade five, I was studying for a science test and feeling very stressed out, thinking I would fail and that this was it for me. Extreme, I know. My mom realized that I was having a meltdown and suggested that I just fail. This shocked the heck out of me, and yet, as I considered her suggestion, I also felt incredible relief.

Was this poor parenting on my mom's part? I don't think so. Her granting me permission to fail gave me the understanding that the world would keep on spinning—that one test was not going to be the end of it for me. And my mom's grander point was this: get used to failing, because life is filled with failure. Failure can have benefits: fine-tuning of a skill through trial and error, encountering a new aspect of yourself ("It was hard but I did it"), and learning what you don't want (just as important as knowing what you do want). Mostly, failure offers the big lesson of survival. After girls step through the failure experience, they can look back with new confidence to say, "I survived!" and "I learned something."

"When I'm not feeling my best, I remind myself that the harder days are what make me stronger." SIMONE BILES

In our attempt to protect a girl (our perfectly natural instinct), we often deny her the chance to stare failure in the face and find a way—her way—to work through it. If we remove failure, we protect our girls in the moment, but we do not protect them from a lifetime of "failure experiences." In taking away their opportunity for failure experience, we are depriving them of the invaluable lessons they need to build their solid foundations, and to build up resilience and perseverance. This is a major disservice. Failure builds character. I'm not saying to leave girls alone to let them figure it out single-handedly; I am saying don't get in the way. Be there, on the sidelines, encouraging and supporting, but not taking over.

So, if instead of sheilding girls from failure, we supported them to think in a new way during moments of pain and suffering, if we equipped them with the skills to thrive despite failure, they could learn to turn setbacks into comebacks. We can help them see there are no wrongs, only lessons learned. Instead of falling apart or getting stuck in the emotion of distress, they can learn that disappointment can be a reason to make a change, and a change for the better! Once they remove the fear of failing and become accustomed to the experience of failing, they take more risks, since they are empowered by the knowledge that when they face failure again, they will know what to do. We want girls to acknowledge and accept their scars and move forward like warriors, ready for battle.

"Never let your failures go to your heart or your successes go to your head." SOICHIRO HONDA

Perhaps failing a test means she has to study differently or ask for help. A fight with a friend may mean it's time for her to learn a new social skill or make a new friend. Hurtful words can inspire her to rise above, "go high," and believe in herself more than ever before. Girls are valuable resources to themselves, with inner knowing, wisdom, skills, talents, and gifts. They can rely on their own character, ability, and strength. They are survivors.

CULTIVATING CONNECTION

Let's talk about:
- What a setback is: think of examples of setbacks she has experienced.
- Failure and what it means: an opportunity to try again.
- Your own setbacks—share with her how you have turned these failures into successes. If you're experiencing setbacks in your relationship with her and need suggestions, see Resource 3 for more on common connection concerns.

- How she has overcome setbacks and failures in the past and what tools she used. Trying again? Taking a break and revisiting an activity later? Changing activities or friends?
- Not dwelling on a setback or a failure, and using this as an opportunity to change and grow.
- The fact that the only real mistake when managing failure is stopping trying to learn and grow, because the mistake is perceived as a reason to give up.
- The benefits of failure, such as learning what she doesn't want or coming up with an even better idea.

Let's try:
- Encouraging her to see the positive in a setback and what she can learn from it. (We learn more from our failures than we do from our successes.) Together reflect on the setback and what happened, and then come up with ideas for how she might approach a task or activity differently.
- Suggesting that she put her energy into creating a comeback. Think of bigger goals and dreams and go for them—this can help her feel that she has choice and can motivate her to try again.
- Playing the rewind game. Ask her to think back on her experience and watch it as if it were a movie. Invite her to consider what she would do differently if she could and what outcome she might have seen instead. Explain to her that while we can't rewind life, we can rewind in our imagination to figure out a new choice. Once she makes a new choice, she will get a different result next time.
- Explaining to her that she has the opportunity to learn and grow every single day—and if learning is ongoing, failure is going to happen because it's necessary for learning.

READ MORE
Very Good Lives, by J.K. Rowling

VIEW MORE
"The Fringe Benefits of Failure," TED Talk by J.K. Rowling

"Embrace the Near Win," TED Talk by Sarah Lewis

"Success, Failure, and the Drive to Keep Creating," TED Talk by Elizabeth Gilbert

- Refraining from swooping in to protect her from failure; instead, help her work *through* failure. Take what she considers a failure and reframe it as growth. If she thinks she said the wrong thing to a friend, encourage her to remember that moment and take time next time to choose her words carefully. Also remind her how common it is to say something hastily.
- Looking at failure as a learning opportunity, and asking "What is the lesson here?"
- Rewarding effort rather than success—this helps her build up resiliency to face failure and to keep trying until she succeeds.
- Teaching her how to accept failure—how to lose or win gracefully, which in turn will help her deal and move on. Accepting failure means accepting all the feelings that are happening because of the failure. Recall the steps for navigating feelings in Chapter 13: noticing and naming feelings, then exploring and expressing them.
- Highlighting mistakes and opportunities to grow—talk with her about your own mistakes, and be a role model.
- Teaching her how to accept feedback in order to learn and grow; to interpret feedback not as a sign of failure but as an opportunity to improve. Teach her how to ask for feedback, and in the style that works best for her. This could mean a positive statement followed by constructive feedback and ending with another positive statement. *I really enjoyed your creative flair in the paragraph you wrote* (positive). *I would love to see more transition phrases* (feedback). *Again, I can see you put in a solid effort. Well done* (positive). You might even call this a "feedback Oreo."

Loving Learning 21

EDUCATION IS ONE of the most impactful ways to build a girl's confidence and help her feel strong and smart. With education, girls acquire the skills and knowledge they need to live rich and meaningful lives, to think for themselves and make important life decisions, and to feel equipped to contribute to society with purpose and passion. It's important that they become active learners, taking responsibility for their own learning process while taking pleasure in it too. To support girl learning, we need to understand how the framework of social emotional learning—which encompasses social, emotional, and academic learning—can help girls apply the knowledge, attitudes, and skills necessary to manage emotions, set goals, feel and show empathy toward others, establish and maintain relationships, and make responsible decisions.[1]

There are five key domains—or "core competencies"—of social emotional learning (SEL). The first is *self-awareness*—identifying and recognizing emotions, self-perception, recognizing strengths, needs, and values, and self-efficacy. The second domain is *social awareness*—perspective taking, empathy, respecting others, and an appreciation of diversity. The third domain is *self-management*—self-motivation, self-discipline, goal setting, organization, stress management, and impulse control. *Relationship management* is the fourth domain—creating and maintaining positive relationships, working cooperatively, asking for and providing help, and navigating conflict. And the fifth domain is *responsible decision making*—problem solving, evaluation, reflection, and taking responsibility.[2]

Research affirms the importance of social emotional learning. When girls feel that their feelings are validated and they share their stories and experiences, they are ready and available to learn. This means that aligning with where they are at and attuning to their emotions is a priority.

"Intellectual growth should commence at birth and cease only at death." ALBERT EINSTEIN

I know from experience that social emotional learning can engage girls in the learning process in an exciting way because it integrates their whole experience: learning, emotions, and relationships. When a girl feels that learning is about more than memorizing what she is told to learn, her ability to absorb and make sense of information becomes about the entire process of learning—including her feelings and effectively managing her emotions; care and empathy for herself and others; making tough choices and decisions; facing and reconciling conflict (her own inner conflict and self-doubt about her abilities, as well as conflicts that may arise with peers); and handling tough situations.

Sure, some girls complain about learning—about going to school and doing homework. But those who find the balance of navigating all the other stuff at school—friends and peer pressure, the stress of tests, and learning new content—deep down enjoy the process, even the stretching. A growing girl will spend a significant portion of her time doing schoolwork, so we need to get behind her and find ways to support her in this process of learning. School is one of the venues where she learns lessons that will serve her as a professional, as a thinker, and as a citizen in the world. At school and at home, she learns how to learn, and if she does it well, it sets the stage for lifelong learning. Lifelong learning can be incorporated into girls' daily life right now as an ongoing, daily habit to be nurtured and cultivated.

Learning to Love Learning

Each and every girl learns in her own way; she has an individual learner profile (learning strengths and areas of growth) and a specific learning style (ability to process and comprehend information). Respecting these differences nurtures her academic development. We need to help girls embrace their learner profile as another aspect of knowing themselves and to see how "smartness" comes in many forms. When we understand how she learns, we are able to work with her in the way she learns best. We need to remember the power of relationships, connection, and emotions in the learning process. When it comes to social emotional learning, relationships matter, because when girls feel safe and secure, they are much more likely to take risks in learning and step into their own potential. Without this kind of close connection in learning, a girl may become more concerned with finding and consolidating the security she needs than feeling free to explore learning new things.

Also, there is a strong connection between learning and how she feels about herself as she learns. The more aware of her feelings she is while learning, and the more calm and positive she is in the learning process, the more she will learn, and the stronger her self-concept will be. What she believes about herself as a learner influences her capacity to take in information and make connections between what she already knows and what she is just learning, and her ability to take risks. The better she feels about herself, the more control she'll feel she has over her learning behaviour and motivation, and the more effectively she will learn.[3] If she thinks she can, she will!

We can instill an appreciation for lifelong learning by showing girls how easy and awesome it is to always be learning—in school and in life. The more open-minded and curious girls are, the more they learn and grow. There is potential to learn every single day, from learning a new word or idea to learning about herself and how she interacts with people and the world around her.

Worth the Effort?

A girl committed to lifelong learning will enjoy many benefits. One: she'll be able to join conversations about many topics and feel that she has something to contribute. She'll be able to connect with others more easily on many topics—no longer will her silence be mistaken for snobbery. Two: she will learn to ask questions and view curiosity as a way to get smarter instead of as a sign of weakness or stupidity. She needs to know she can be brave enough to wonder. Three: she will be interested in learning—whether at school or elsewhere. Once she taps into the notion of "I can make anything interesting if I put in some time and effort," she understands that engagement can come from inside her and is not contingent on her teacher or the school curriculum. Four: she can feel like a competent and capable learner.

When girls embrace learning as a daily practice, they learn to pay attention to the world around them, and they learn the invaluable lesson of being responsible for their knowledge. They also realize that learning can be exciting and a tremendous source of power. The more competent girls feel, the more confident they feel. And with knowledge comes inner power and wisdom.

Now let's take a look at two fundamental tools for lifelong learning: expanding vocabulary and asking questions.

Expanding Vocabulary, Expanding Knowledge

When I was young, I fell in love with words. I remember I shared an observation with my dad about another person, and he called me "astute." I had no idea what it meant but I knew it was a compliment. After I learned the definition of "astute," I understood my dad was telling me I could accurately assess a person. I got hooked on language learning and have prioritized building my vocabulary ever since. The compliment, of course, encouraged my interest in words!

By learning vocabulary—new words—girls gain the tools to learn new concepts and to become better thinkers in the process. Words are the foundation for ideas. Make learning vocabulary a daily habit for her and convey the importance of knowing a variety of words. It starts with encouraging her to ask the question "What does the word —— mean?" You may be surprised by how much she starts to ask about. And once she starts asking, she is learning, and she's equipping herself with a strategy for life. Every new subject area—whether it's math, cooking, or fashion—has its specific language.

Let's say you are talking about computers, and she asks you what the word "download" means. This can become a teachable moment—to define the word "download" and to explain some basics of technological communication, best practices in file management, or the cost of cell phone data plans. She may have a working knowledge of words but not be able to precisely define them. Specific word learning can build her intelligence.

Curiosity Is Key: Asking Questions

Girls tend to listen more than they speak. They can be particularly shy and passive in the classroom, preferring to remain in the dark rather than risk the embarrassment of asking a "dumb" question. So we can practise the skill of asking questions with her in her safe space.

Start by prompting her to ask simple questions, often referred to as the five Ws: who, what, when, where, and why? Then move on to more challenging questions—"Why not," "What would happen if?" and "What else?" Her asking questions and being curious is an entry point into meaningful conversation. And her asking questions about what she sees and the world around her helps her become informed. Girls need to know that asking questions isn't a sign of stupidity because they don't know something, but a sign of intelligence because they know when they don't know, and so need to find out.

Both expanding vocabulary and asking questions are fundamental learning tools that become the cornerstones of girls' thinking skills. With practice—learning is a life skill that requires daily attention and effort—and success, these skills become part of her daily rhythms.

Now that we've explored the two fundamental tools for lifelong learning, let's take a look at a couple of basic learning strategies.

Staying Focused

Focus and attention are key for effective learning and information processing. Girls cannot learn without them. If you have the chance to peek in on her classroom, you'll see a cornucopia of competing attention-getters—and lots of wandering eyes, fidgeting, wiggling bodies, and secretive texting. In short, girls are paying less and less attention in classrooms everywhere, and as a result are not getting all the information they need, including instructions and core content. So we need to assist girls in managing distractions, first by reminding them of the expectations of focus and what focus looks like: eye contact or looking, still hands and feet, sitting up tall (to help with efficient breathing); and second, putting all tempting distractions away. When you notice that a girl is distracted or zoning out, bring it to her attention, to help her bring her focus back.

Also, we need to remind girls that a job worth doing is one worth doing well, and this means doing one task at a time. So forget multi-tasking; single-tasking is the only way to go (see Chapter 6 for more on mindfulness). When girls pride themselves on doing many tasks at one time, their attention is divided and each task suffers in quality. Doing one task with full attention and then moving on to the next task increases the likelihood of efficiency and requires less time overall. So the next time a girl is doing her homework while watching Netflix and messaging a friend, remind her to devote her full attention to *one* task, fully enjoy it, and then choose the next task to focus on.

Making It Meaningful

The second strategy involves staying engaged. Let's face it—sometimes school is boring. Sometimes a documentary a girl thinks is going to be interesting turns out to be about something that doesn't apply to her at all. Girls find it difficult to learn when they feel that the information is irrelevant to them. I'm sure you have heard complaints about how boring a subject or teacher is. But we can empower girls to make meaning on their own.

This may translate into encouraging her to ask questions; make connections between topics to find associations related to her memories of a topic; chunk information together into meaningful categories; think about what she is learning—reflective learning—in order to make connections to what she already knows, instead of rushing to finish; and do extra research on a topic that interests her. A little time spent researching can make a big difference in understanding. The more work she does, the better her attention and the more likely she is to learn because the information matters to her. This may sound like a lot of work, but it is the difference between being a passive learner (simply sitting and receiving information) and being an active learner (engaging in a lesson, participating, and doing something with what she is learning). And taking responsibility for making her own meaning can suddenly make any subject relevant, thereby making it more engaging.

Active Learners

So, we now know that the state of staying engaged and being responsible for making new information meaningful is considered "active learning." Active learners do not sit and wait to be given knowledge, but take an active role in the learning process. This can mean being prepared with supplies to take part or take notes, asking questions, mind mapping (a visual thinking tool to show the interconnection between ideas and concepts), coming up with acronyms for memory work, creating cue cards for vocabulary, or drawing pictures—whatever works for her. And it involves paying attention and thinking *while* learning. I like to use the questions "What do you already know about this topic?" (to stimulate thought) and "How can you connect this new information to knowledge you already have?" When girls are thinking and connecting *while* they learn, they'll stay interested and engaged, increasing the likelihood of understanding.

"Learning how to learn is one of the most important skills in life." NORMA FAUZIYAH

Being an active learner also means not blaming the teacher, the school, or the subject. So watch your own language, and check in if you are placing blame on others for her learning. It's all too easy to blame the "boring" teacher or the "inadequate" school. Yes, some teachers and schools are better than others. However, blaming becomes an excuse for not putting in the effort.

Being an active learner requires girls to have grit: the resolve to work hard and dig deep, no matter what, and to see that their efforts are requisite for their own successes. The truth girls need to know is that there are no quick fixes, shortcuts, or easy answers in life, especially when it comes to becoming a stronger learner. Growth requires time, practice, and patience, and growth demands grit!

Voracious Reading

The most successful learners are active readers. They read anything and everything! They seek knowledge and, by doing so, they learn new words, how to think (on both a literal level and an interpretive level), how to write and put ideas together in different ways, and how to articulate their thoughts. Readers learn how to understand, interpret, analyze, synthesize, and summarize information. Encourage girls to read and to make reading a priority and daily habit. Consider reading print books over reading onscreen, as research suggests that print reading enhances the sensory experience and therefore the comprehension.[4] Ask questions to encourage them to reflect on and then to share what they've read and provide an opinion. If they give the bare minimum, ask "What else?" to encourage insights and ideas.

Start Now

Successful learners do not procrastinate. How many times have you learned that your daughter has a project only the night before it's due, or that she has a test *the next day*? Leaving things this late can cause unnecessary anxiety and stress for a girl, as she knows it's not enough prep time to do a good job. "Start now" is always good advice: that way, there is enough time to complete an assignment. Doing a little work toward a project or studying every single day before test day is often enough for the brain to process the information and for tasks to evolve and develop. Research supports this technique of spaced learning and studying.[5] When girls start working right away instead of procrastinating, they place themselves in a position of strength. They feel good about taking a step, and this may motivate them to then take another step. Also, when anxiety is decreased, work quality often rises.

If a girl struggles with procrastination, check in with her as to *why* she is procrastinating. Common reasons are fear and insecurity, feeling ill-equipped, not being clear on instructions, and

READ MORE

The Learning Coach Approach, by Linda Dobson

Raising Lifelong Learners, by Lucy Calkins with Lydia Bellino

Studying, Test Taking, and Getting Good Grades, by Susanna Palomares and Dianne Schilling

Turnaround Tools for the Teenage Brain, by Eric Jensen and Carole Snider

disinterest. It's rare that a girl doesn't want to do well on a task; it's much more likely that she just doesn't know how to get started.

CULTIVATING CONNECTION

Let's talk about:

- How learning is important at school, and how she can learn on her own—looking up anything that she is interested in.
- The value of lifelong learning for her own individual personal best.
- Making meaningful connections between what she already knows and new information. Start with what she already knows about a subject. She usually knows at least one fact about a topic, even if it is only her familiarity with one key word—start here to build confidence and increase interest and motivation.
- The value of reading and finding books she loves to read.

Let's try:

- Creating a chart of learning strengths and areas of growth. Ask her how she thinks she learns best. Consider: listening and following directions, vocabulary, writing, mathematics, reading, reading comprehension, note taking, and drawing. Help her see that she has both strengths and areas of growth, and that this is another aspect of her that makes her unique.
- Making learning more meaningful by taking advantage of everyday learning opportunities in her life: preparing recipes (for nutrition, math, and organization), grocery shopping (for budgeting, recognizing the value of money,

and planning), house cleaning (for systematic thinking, organization, and time management), and banking (for financial planning and math).

- Providing success in learning possibilities—and the positive emotions that go with this—outside of school. This might be learning about a sports teams she loves, about her favourite author, or more about her most prized animal. Follow her curiosities and interests. Creatively link learning on her own with the skills she needs to complete schoolwork.

- Creating a book for recording and defining new vocabulary. Set a goal, such as twenty-five words per week. Choose themes, and ask her to choose some of them too (for example, words about transit, cooking, politics, or sports).

- Helping her ask her own questions: take time to brainstorm learning questions. Write each on a cue card and encourage her to spread these cards out when she is reading or doing homework. For instance:

  > *What do I already know about this topic?*
  > *What connections can I make between what I am learning and my own experiences?*
  > *How can I learn more about this topic for better understanding?*
  > *Why is this information important to know?*

- Practising "thinking on her feet." This is a tough one for many girls, who freeze when asked a question, or to make a contribution in class. She may feel her anxiety spike, or she may be flooded with self-doubt. Help her think more quickly by giving her a topic and asking her to make one comment on the topic. Start easy with what she knows, and then begin to ask more learning-related topics. She can say anything, and

VIEW MORE
www.quizlet
.com

TRY THIS APP
Word of
the Day

everything is acceptable. The purpose is for her to practise quick thinking and to become more confident and comfortable with those on-the-spot moments.

- Helping her make learning fun by setting up games to play at homework time. For example, ask her to write down on small pieces of paper each of the assignments or portions of assignments she has to complete. Fold up the papers and place them in a lunch bag or baseball hat. One by one, let her pick a piece of paper. When she has completed the task listed on the paper, she gets to decide on a five-minute break activity, such as running around the house, listening and dancing to a song, or a quick snack.

- Addressing procrastination. Start with a "definition" of the word—putting some jobs off until later so that she can do fun or easier jobs first. Brainstorm and record reasons for procrastination, and ask her to choose those that match her reasons. Perhaps it's fear of not understanding, disinterest or boredom, not knowing how to start, or feeling that there won't be enough time to complete the work. Whatever the reasons are, it is important to know and then address each. For instance, if she doesn't know how to start, help her write a list of all the steps and then put them in order. Teach her the habit of doing a task immediately and being rewarded with peace of mind and playtime or downtime without worry.

See Resource 4 for tips for homework and studying.

Learning for Life   22

ONCE A GIRL has an interest in lifelong learning, there are several ways in which we can continue to encourage her to embrace learning. Schools may define success by standardized test results, post-secondary admissions, and academic performance. She may be accustomed to defining success by grades earned on a report card and teacher approval. Success, in my opinion, is when a girl has a positive attitude toward learning and is willing to put in the effort to learn and grow.

We can help girls be *successful* learners, first, by broadening the definition of success and having her define what a "successful learner" means to her. Successful learners know that they get to decide what success looks like. These learners also attribute their successes to their own efforts and hard work, not luck. Not all girls perform well on tests, earn high grades, understand on their first try, or learn in traditional ways. School doesn't "fit" every learner. Until the educational system is reformed to accommodate a diversity of students, and those kids who think *way* outside the box, we can help girls define successful learning on their own terms.

And when a girl learns how to learn, investigates her unique learner profile (learning strengths and areas of growth), and takes responsibility for being an active, engaged participant in her learning, she becomes a *strong* learner. There is no stopping her. She can learn anything. With a positive attitude and positive self-talk, persistent effort, and meaningful connections to what they learn, girls feel equipped and prepared for optimal academic growth.

You will recognize a strong learner because she starts to articulate her ideas and opinions and contribute to the conversation, whether in the car with you or at the dining-room table. She will ask questions because she now knows it's her right and responsibility, and one of the greatest ways to empower herself with knowledge. A strong learner will start to make connections between what you say and what she is learning at school, blending new information and what she already knows. She may surprise you; she may call you on contradictions you express or start fact checking what you say.

More Than One Kind of Smart

In his theory of multiple intelligences, developmental psychologist Howard Gardner asserts that there are nine types of intelligence: musical-rhythmic, visual-spatial, verbal-linguistic, logical-mathematical, bodily-kinesthetic, interpersonal, intrapersonal, naturalistic, and existential.[1] Gardner emphasizes that intelligence is not compartmentalized into one kind of smart, and that people have a unique blend of skills and capabilities. Girls are easily frustrated when they aren't academically talented, and are often unable to see that their talents may come in other ways, such as being a fantastic artist or having street smarts. Gardner's theory is a great reminder to us all not to limit ourselves to any one kind of intelligence.

What's Her Learning Style?

As you come to understand the types of intelligences, explore ways to develop each. Walter Burke Barbe, an American education educator who developed the model to identify visual, auditory, and kinesthetic (VAK) learners, proposes that each learner has a dominant sense when it comes to how best to learn. He proposes three basic modalities for learning, as noted above: visual, auditory, and tactile/kinesthetic.[2]

Visual learners need to see what they are learning. They benefit from any type of visual aid—a chart, diagram, mind map, picture, video, handout. They also need to see the speaker, so it's best if visual learners sit at the front of the classroom.

Auditory learners learn best by hearing incoming information. This means listening to a lesson and audiobooks, being involved in discussion groups, and presenting to their peers. They also learn well using songs and rhymes.

"If a child can't learn the way we teach, maybe we should teach the way they learn." IGNACIO ESTRADA

Finally, kinesthetic (tactile or touch-oriented) learners learn best by using their bodies—they need to be physically involved. This might include drawing, doodling, and taking notes, as well as doing arts-and-crafts projects and hands-on tasks. Kinesthetic learners also need to move their bodies while learning—something not every classroom environment allows for. Gum chewing, squeezing a stress ball, pacing back and forth, wiggling in their seat, and bouncing on a yoga ball all help these types of learners stay engaged.

Advocacy here is essential: girls need to know that they can ask for what they need to accommodate their learning needs. And because everyone learns differently, thanks to their unique learning profile, life experiences, and core competencies and skill set, we need to meet girls where they are and support them from that place. Teach her the concept of learning to learn. Find out what she knows, then add new knowledge.

No Limits to Learning

Ultimately, if girls aren't strong in one kind of intelligence or in one style of learning, they can still grow, with effort. There are no limits to learning. Research supports the notion that our brains are plastic, meaning they can create new cells and pathways. Changing the brain takes mental preparation, targeted intervention, repetition, and practice. We all have the potential to change our brains.

According to Drs. Daniel J. Siegel and Tina Payne Bryson in *The Whole-Brain Child*, it's essential to consider the integration of left brain and right brain. The authors say this about the two hemispheres: "Your left brain loves and desires order. It is *logical*, *literal*, *linguistic* (it likes words), and *linear* (it puts things in a sequence or order)... The right brain, on the other hand, is holistic and nonverbal, sending and receiving signals that allow us to communicate, such as facial expressions, eye contact, tone of voice, posture, and gestures. Instead of details and order, our right brain cares about the big picture—the meaning and feel of an experience—and specializes in images, emotions, and personal memories."[3]

With this knowledge, we have another opportunity to teach girls to diversify their learning. The more integration that occurs between the two hemispheres, the more interesting learning can be, and the more deep processing is happening. The two hemispheres working together in *horizontal integration* creates a sense of harmony in the brain—and this can help girls live balanced, meaningful, and creative lives. This research helps us understand the importance of teaching the "big picture" first, before filling in the details. Think of putting a jigsaw puzzle together as a child. Chances are you put together the frame first, then placed the other pieces inside the frame. You had a system. Similarly, girls benefit from the structure of a concept—the big picture—as the foundation for learning the details.

Many girls I've worked with have designations for giftedness, a learning disability, a combination of giftedness and a learning disability, autism spectrum disorder (ASD), sensory processing disorder (SPD), or a moderate to profound intellectual disability. I have seen first-hand how their consistent hard work has pushed them to develop their weaker areas and manage their learning challenges. And since girls are natural pleasers and rule followers, they often make ideal students. Generally, they listen well, they follow directions, they work hard, and they complete their tasks. However, the downside is that they may look like they're learning more than they actually are: as mentioned in Chapter 6, girls are underdiagnosed for learning difficulties and specifically for ADD and ADHD. If you suspect that this is the case with your girl, or you'd like to know more about how she learns best, her processing speed and efficiency, and her learning potential, seek professional guidance. I strongly recommend a psychoeducational or learning assessment. With data about a girl's brain and learning efficiency and potential, it's much easier to make informed decisions about her individualized education plan and ways to further support her. In my work with girls, I find that the reports that emerge from these assessments help me support girls in specific and customized ways.

Keep It Fresh

To help girls stay mentally sharp, we can encourage them to learn something every day, and to do so in a variety of ways—perhaps by reading news articles online or listening to the news, learning a few new vocabulary terms, or simply asking questions and engaging in meaningful dialogue. (You may think reading the news is an adults-only activity, but I find it to be a great learning tool for vocabulary, concepts, connecting in conversations, and building awareness of what's happening in the world.) Mental clarity and sharpness can also be gained through physical activities such as yoga, soccer, and martial arts. Sports are risks and can open a

READ MORE

Help Your Child Succeed at School, by Jonathan Hancock

Sensational Kids: Hope and Help for Children with Sensory Processing Disorder (SPD), by Dr. Lucy Jane Miller

The Whole-Brain Child, by Dr. Daniel J. Siegel and Dr. Tina Payne Bryson

girl up to an entirely new kind of learning: cooperation, competition, learning how to win and lose, and managing emotions. Some girls love logic games and puzzles. Whatever she chooses to learn, the key is consistency and variety—switching up activities to prevent the "I'm bored." Brains also need adequate sleep, hydration, and nutritious food to stay focused and alert. And when mentally taxed, a "brain break" is in order. Switching gears to fun and mindless activities allows the brain to rest.

Learning is also much more interesting when it includes as many styles as possible. Think multi-modal and multi-sensory—meaning the more parts of the brain and body we can involve in the learning and teaching process, the better. Not all classrooms can accommodate each individual learning need (though it's worth asking), but we can teach girls to use their learning styles when studying or doing homework. So suggest she uses her learning strength *and* diversify her learning styles. This could involve reading her notes out loud while walking around her room and listening to soft, soothing background music. Not only will she learn more effectively, but she might just have fun in the process. Variety and stimulation are key.

CULTIVATING CONNECTION

Let's talk about:
- What a being a successful learner means to her. On a piece of paper, draw a stick figure in the middle, and then ask her to brainstorm by writing all over the page what a successful learner looks like, focusing on what she can *do* to learn better (pay attention, organize her supplies, ask more questions, review homework after school, ask for help). You might also talk about what an unsuccessful learner looks

like (not paying attention, being distracted by objects or her own thoughts, putting jobs off until later, not asking for help).

- The different learning styles: visual, auditory, and tactile/kinesthetic.
- How she likes to learn, and how she feels she learns best.

Let's try:

- Creating a chart with three headings: "Visual," "Auditory," and "Tactile/Kinesthetic." Work together to write out examples of each of these learning styles. Perhaps visual learning includes reading and handouts; auditory learning, listening to audiobooks and discussing learning topics; tactile and kinesthetic, moving while memorizing facts and doing hands-on projects and crafts.
- Encouraging her to be an active learner: attentive and engaged. This may be as simple as having eye contact with the instructor or sitting at the front of the class. Also consider using sensory items that engage her body—chewing gum, a bouncy ball, a stress ball—or giving her permission to wiggle.
- Trying activities that combine all three learning styles and having some fun! Read aloud from a textbook while walking around the room. Write out the key ideas on cue cards. Ask her for another idea for how to combine all three learning styles.
- Helping her attribute her own successes—no matter how big or small—to her efforts and hard work, not luck.
- Encouraging her to learn new things outside of the school curriculum. She could take up playing a musical instrument, spend time in nature to gain knowledge about plants and animals, try a new board game, or learn a new language.

VIEW MORE
www.mindware.com

www.cogmed.com

www.luminosity.com

www.scholastic.com/100books/

TRY THESE APPS
AB Maths

Duolingo (for language)

Magic Jigsaw Puzzles

News-O-Matic (current events for kids)

Unblock Me

23 Scattered and Smart

I HAVE HEARD this story so many times, I've lost count, but it is worth telling. It goes something like this: *My daughter came to me last Wednesday at 9 p.m. in tears and complete disarray. Thinking there had been a major catastrophe in her world, like her best friend was moving to another city, or she received a failing grade, I was informed she had a big social studies project due Thursday—as in, the next day. So here we are, late at night, just as I was hoping to have a bath and unwind with a good book. But now I'm thrown this curveball. It gets worse. Upon asking her where her textbook is and what exactly the assignment requires, I find out that the materials she needs are at school, and although she wrote down the steps for the project, these are in her planner which is—you guessed it—at school too!*

As I say, these kinds of stories are common and consistent—I hear them all the time. Is a growing girl responsible for her school work? Yes. Is she responsible for her brain? Well, yes and no. Yes, she has to learn to get her homework done on time and ask for help if she needs it. At the same time, we need to be aware that her brain is also growing and not yet fully developed. This means she may struggle with some or many executive functioning skills. (If you haven't heard this buzzword before, don't worry.)

The executive functioning skills, or EF skills, are a set of mental processes that direct a student's thoughts, actions, and emotions, especially through active problem solving and decision making. These functioning skills include thinking, planning, evaluating, and responding to tasks while allowing for cognitive flexibility and for controlled, effortful processing, and they are foundational skills for learning.

When girls learn what the executive functioning skills are and become strong managers of them, they develop greater self-aware-ness as learners and build greater capacity to manage the tasks of organizing and systematizing new material. In short, as girls increase their understanding of the executive functioning skills, they increase their learning success. This is something they can actively work on, and we can actively support.

"Everybody is a genius. But if you judge a fish by its ability to climb a tree, it will live its whole life believing that it's stupid." ALBERT EINSTEIN

In a growing girl's brain, the prefrontal cortex (home of the executive functioning skills) is the last to develop, including her time management, organization skills, decision making, and judgment. However, this does not mean she can't develop or even master these skills. In fact, many girls are very strong in these skills. Thanks to the emerging science of brain plasticity, we know that the brain can develop new neural pathways with . . . *experience.* This means we can teach girls the executive functioning skills, and that there is hope for a seemingly scattered girl to show how smart she can be!

With practice and repetition, and the enormous potential to build up brain efficiency, the executive functioning skills can be strengthened. With this in mind, here are brief descriptions of these skills. Ideas to support a girl's growth in the executive func-tioning skills follow in the Cultivating Connection box below.

Response inhibition is the capacity to think before acting. This ability to resist the urge to be impulsive and say or do something without thinking allows her time to evaluate a situation and how her behaviour might impact it. *Working memory* is the ability to keep key information in mind while performing complex tasks, such as note taking or remembering instructions. *Emotional control* is managing emotions and keeping feelings in check, so as to respond rather than react to situations, and to recalibrate when something doesn't go one's way. *Attention* is the capacity to keep focused on a situation or task in spite of distractions, fatigue, or boredom. *Task initiation* is the ability to know how to get started and to avoid the pitfalls of procrastination. *Planning and prioritizing* is the ability to create a road map to reach a goal or complete a task, and to know which steps or tasks are most important. *Organization* is the creation and maintenance of systems to keep track of information or materials—from handouts to cell phones to her own train of thought. *Time management* includes estimating how much time she has, how she chooses to allocate it, and how to stay within time limits and deadlines. It also involves a sense that time is important. *Goal-directed persistence* is the ability to have a goal, follow through to the completion of the goal, and not be put off or distracted by competing interests, as well as to have persistence in the face of adversity. *Flexibility and shifting* is the ability to revise plans in the face of obstacles, setbacks, new information, or mistakes, and to learn to think about things from many angles. *Metacognition and self-monitoring* together are the skill of standing back to check in with herself about how she is doing, and to be realistic about her progress and growth.

As you can imagine, it would be especially difficult for a girl to manage these skills when dysregulated or, in other words, overwhelmed, overstressed, and out of sorts. So when it comes to her learning these skills, we need to consider *her* context: she may be addicted to her screen, lacking in sleep or proper nutrition, or in the midst of escalating social concerns, which makes practicing these skills near impossible! So it is important that she include self-regulation—the ability to calm down, slow down, and guide one's own thoughts, feelings, and behaviours in order to regulate emotions and stress—in addition to mindfulness, when learning the executive functioning skills.

So, the next time you are taken by surprise with "It's due tomorrow and I haven't started yet," take a minute to gain your composure. Breathe. And know that the problem is one that can be addressed and prevented by exploring ways to help her become less scattered and much stronger in her executive functioning skills.

CULTIVATING CONNECTION

Let's talk about:

- What executive functioning means—her ability to plan, organize, and think ahead; to solve problems and make decisions.
- The various examples of executive functioning skills and which ones she feels are her strengths and areas of growth.

Let's try:

- Guiding her to express and navigate her emotions, and to self-regulate in order to calm herself down by deep breathing and checking in with her body.
- Encouraging her to wait three seconds before speaking.
- Practising learning rote memory work by repeating two pieces of information at a time, and increasing the number of pieces over time.
- Being explicit about your expectations of her efforts to focus

READ MORE
Fish in a Tree, by Lynda Mullaly Hunt

Late, Lost, and Unprepared: A Parents' Guide to Helping Children with Executive Functioning, by Joyce Cooper-Kahn

No Mind Left Behind: Understanding and Fostering Executive Control, by Adam J. Cox

Smart but Scattered, by Peg Dawson and Richard Guare

and concentrate. Focus includes eye contact, sitting up tall, looking and learning, and limiting distractions (especially thoughts and devices), as best she can.

- Using a calendar or daily planner to record all tasks and due dates—have her list the jobs she needs to do in order of importance or difficulty.

- Having all supplies ready and having her organize key areas such as her desk, backpack, and locker for five minutes each day.

- Guessing how long a task should take and then noting how long it does take—use a clock, watch, or timer to keep track of the time.

- Writing out goals and making them visible—list all sub-goals and urge her to begin striving for them immediately, one small action step at a time.

- Planning for changes and setbacks by discussing backup plans and options for when changes do occur—be prepared for change.

- Asking her questions to promote awareness of her own learning process and progress: "How are you doing? What did you do well? What could you improve on? How do you feel you are growing?"

- Trying activities that promote the development of executive functioning skills: music, singing, dance, team sports, card games, puzzles, theatre, musical theatre, strategy games, logic puzzles.

Tips for Reducing Test Anxiety

Without a doubt, tests can cause a great deal of anxiety. One of the best ways to face the fear of tests head-on is to prepare and practise beforehand, and to stay calm and in control during the test. To that end:

- Ask her about what else besides the upcoming test specifically worries her about school.
- Ask her how she feels before, during, and after a test.
- Prompt her to prepare, plan, and organize all her study materials (you'd be surprised by how many times materials that she needs are missing).
- Suggest that she finds out the format of the test (multiple choice, matching, short answer, essay?), so that she knows how best to study.
- Encourage her to space out her studying over time to improve retention of the material, and to take several breaks as she studies.
- Remind her of the importance of preparation and practice (active learning) and of making studying fun with a variety of study techniques (using cue cards, rewriting notes, reciting information aloud, creating a mock test).
- Remind her to keep a positive attitude before, during, and after a test.
- Ask her to choose different physical activities she can do between studying times—a run, a walk, or a few jumping jacks—to reduce stress.
- Remind her to get a good night's sleep before the test, and to eat a nutritious breakfast on test day.

What's Ahead? Planning and Preparing for the Future

24

GIRLS WHO PREPARE and plan for the future are generally more independent and responsible and far less anxious than those who don't. I'm not talking here about long-range, future thinking. We can probably all agree that dwelling on the distant future can be cause for concern. A young girl may get freaked out if she starts thinking about what is to come for her: getting her driver's licence, applying to universities, moving out on her own. No, I am talking about her future as in her week ahead and what's on her schedule. When girls plan and prepare for themselves—the ongoing process of thinking ahead—they are less filled with worry and can focus on the wonder instead. Rather than worrying, "What if I am not successful in life?" she can wonder, "In what way will I succeed in my life?"

A girl who has no plan—who stumbles her way through life—is constantly "surprised" when she can't find an important project or when she misplaces her backpack yet again. She is ill-prepared for what is to come and often feels terribly out of control and out of sync with her peers. She may even decide to play the part of the "cool girl," masquerading as a girl who couldn't care less, when really she simply doesn't yet know the how-to of organizing herself. If you recall from the previous chapter, most likely she is struggling with her executive functioning skills, which are foundational for all other skills and meaning-making.

When we teach girls to plan, prepare, and think ahead (even a little), and to be organized, we also teach them self-management and self-confidence. And we teach girls to better regulate their stress—feeling "too busy" can be quickly placated by spending some time planning with a calendar—by deciding when to do what task, in what order. In short, girls with a plan are often more balanced, calm, and happy. In the words of Maria Menounos, in her book *The EveryGirl's Guide to Life*, "Disorganization inhibits happiness and increases stress and chances for failure."[1]

"Being organized is just a matter of putting in some extra time and effort, which, again, save you time and effort in the long run." MARIA MENOUNOS

The foundation of the executive functioning skill of planning and preparing for her future—whether it's tomorrow, next week, or next year—is being organized, and this is best done with some basic tools: a calendar, a day planner, and sticky notes (either physical materials or on a smartphone). Take ten-year-old Jada, for example, who is in the habit of preparing: she takes time each day to look at her school planner. She can ensure, all by herself, that she has completed her homework, and she can get ready for the next day by packing her backpack. She may need clothes for gym class, money for a hot lunch, and a signed permission slip for an upcoming field trip. By taking a little bit of time to organize herself, Jada can have peace of mind that she's ready, thereby limiting surprises and forgetfulness.

I know what you might be thinking—"This *sounds* great in theory, but how do I get my girl to actually want to be planned and prepared, when she can barely remember to brush her teeth in

READ MORE

The Every-Girl's Guide to Life, by Maria Menounos

the morning?" Or what if a girl is a procrastinator and wants to put everything off until "tomorrow"? What if asking her to do any task has become such hard work, you've stopped trying? What if she simply isn't interested in preparing?

Well, you start by discussing what being organized could look like for her, and you ask questions such as "What is coming up for you that you can get ready for right now?" Then you do it *with* her—at first—helping her plan a project, writing a homework to-do list, or creating a grocery list for Saturday shopping, which helps make the abstract idea of preparation become tangible and possible. Spend time communicating to her the benefits of preparing: lower stress and anxiety, getting more completed, and even increased health, happiness, and quality of life. Experiencing the effects of being prepared and organized, and realizing how much she can get accomplished when she plans her day, may motivate her more than ever. And you can slide out of your hand-holder role into the role of coach, to keep her on track and to encourage her to stay organized, planned, and prepared. Everyone can benefit from preparation coaching—even strong girls!

CULTIVATING CONNECTION

Let's talk about:

- The importance of planning, preparation, and organization.
- What she will feel like if she plans, prepares, and organizes herself and her belongings ahead of time.
- What she can do with all the time she is earning for herself by planning and preparing.

Let's try:

- Showing her how to use calendars, school planners, and reminder notes; helping her write out to-do lists.
- Asking her "What is coming up for you that you can get ready for right now?"
- Investing in organizing supplies: storage bins, baskets, shelves, school supplies.
- Teaching her that "everything has a place, and there's a place for everything," and guiding her to clean up after herself, putting items such as her backpack, cell phone, and clothing in their appropriate places.
- Spending fifteen minutes together (at least at first) each night packing a lunch and her backpack for school the next day.

Who's in Charge? Choices and Decision Making

25

GIRLS TODAY HAVE more choices than in any other generation. They have a plethora of choices of: name brands and labels, courses at school, after-school activities and groups to join, and, later, careers and professional interests to pursue. They also must make daily decisions about what to say, how to act, and how to deal with miscommunications. Ironically, girls are more stressed out by these choices than ever before. Journalism professor Barbara Kelley, in *Psychology Today*, notices a burgeoning trend among her female students: "They were bright, successful, highly motivated—and terribly confused. Raised with great expectations by parents who told them they could do anything, they worked hard, earned top grades, polished their resumes, began impressive careers, then collapsed in metaphysical uncertainty, anxious and overwhelmed."[1] Here, we can see that too much choice can be stressful and lead to confusion rather than clarity.

Yet, for some girls, choice brings a sense of entitlement. But choice is not something every girl around the globe has, unfortunately. I believe that our girls need to know they are fortunate. And they need to know that choices—whether it's to wear an appropriate or a revealing outfit, to be kind to a friend or mean, or to stick with a class or activity when the going gets tough or drop it—have consequences. They need to take responsibility for what they choose, and they need to know that their choices mould their characters and the types of people they will become.

How does a girl gain clarity on her choices and know that a decision is right for her? This is where you can help her sort through uncertainty and figure out how to make choices and decisions that fit who she is and what she needs at that time. There is no right answer in the absolute sense, but there is a right answer for her, gained only in the process of checking in with herself—with her body, feelings, and thoughts—and being honest with and true to herself, meeting herself with understanding and self-compassion, being brave enough to express herself clearly and with confidence, and voicing her opinion because she has a voice and she gets to use it.

"One's philosophy is not best expressed in words. It is expressed in the choices one makes. And the choices we make are ultimately our responsibility." **ELEANOR ROOSEVELT**

Girls are typically told all day what to do—from homework to after-school chores—so they can really benefit from having some choice and say in the matter. Choice empowers girls, and with power they feel strong on the inside. So let's provide them with some choice, to include them in the decision-making process. It can be simple, such as "Do you want spaghetti or pizza for dinner?" or more complex, such as "Do you want to tell me about your day so I can help you through it, or do you want to go for ice cream and talk about your day when you're ready?" By giving girls choice, we empower them to take ownership and start to build a sense of self-worth and independent thinking. Today, we are asking them to choose after we provide options. Later, they will come up with their own options from which to make their own choices. As they make more and more choices, their characters begin to take shape. It is through the decision-making process that we can teach girls the most about integrity, honesty, independence, loyalty, determination, and courage.

"I don't lose. I either win or I learn." NELSON MANDELA

Choice or decisions can be further supported by conversations about making good choices. A little thinking ahead, exploring, and brainstorming can help girls see all the factors going into a decision, as well as the possible outcomes. This can guide girls to make healthy and informed decisions. When a girl makes a decision that brings a positive result, affirm her decision—even celebrate it. Also be prepared for when she makes a decision that has a negative outcome—seize it as an opportunity for her to reflect, evaluate, and reconsider for next time. But, ultimately, girls need to know that there is no such thing as a bad decision; rather, all decisions are opportunities to grow and learn. As the saying goes, "Nothing ventured, nothing gained."

CULTIVATING CONNECTION

Let's talk about:
- Choices and decisions she has made that she feels proud of and happy about.
- Choices and decisions she has made that she thinks she could improve on.
- The fact that she always has choice; it's about making the best choice for herself.

- The fact that choice doesn't always have to be an *either or*; by finding a compromise it can be *both and*.

Let's try:
- Giving her opportunities to practise making choices and thinking for herself. For example, provide options for dinner, or let her choose a relative's birthday gift. Ask her how she made her choices.
- Creating, together, a list of pros and cons of possible decisions and outcomes. For example, the pros and cons of going on a school camping trip that she may be feeling fearful about. What are the pros? (For example, fun and time with friends outside of school.) What are the cons? (For example, a new environment, sleeping in a new bed, not knowing what may happen.) Have her look at both the pros and the cons and decide what she wants to do, knowing she has your full support and that if she doesn't go this time, going next time is an option.
- Asking how she wants to handle a problem she's encountering. If she will be missing school to go on a band trip, ask her what she feels she needs to do to deal with her absence. Come up with as many ideas as possible, and don't discount any idea she suggests. Together, look at the options and explore possible outcomes of each. Then, ask her what she feels is the best answer (this might even be a combination of options). Ask her how she feels when she makes that choice and what it feels like to trust herself.
- Affirming moments when she makes a healthy decision, chooses to express her needs, or talks about herself using positive and confident language.

READ MORE
Mindfulness for Teen Anxiety, by Christopher Willard

The Self-Esteem Workbook for Teens, by Lisa M. Schab

Motivation:

26 Let's Get Moving

A QUESTION I AM frequently asked is "How do I motivate my daughter?" It may be about motivating her to do her homework without your having to tell her to do it, or to do chores around the house, or any number of things. The answer is that you can't. *You* cannot motivate the girl in your life to do anything. Motivation occurs naturally in kids until about age seven, then they need to learn the skill of self-motivation.

Motivation, or the desire to act or move, takes two forms: intrinsic and extrinsic. Intrinsic motivation is the desire to do something for the sake of activity itself. This means that sometimes girls will do an activity because it feels good, and sometimes they will do an activity because they get something out of it. For example, a girl may be motivated to go horseback riding because she loves the feeling of being on a horse and the freedom she experiences practising jumps. Extrinsic motivation is the desire to do an activity for an external reward. A girl may work hard so that she earns good grades.

But what about the girl who isn't motivated? You can *try* to motivate her. And she may even temporarily appease you, but you can be certain that you will also receive her resentment in the form of eye rolling or sighs of exasperation, or worse, as the push-pull that transpires turns into a power struggle. I understand the strong desire to see girls choose motivation over stagnation. We want the best for them, and we want them to make positive choices for themselves. In essence, we want girls to be self-motivated. But the best way we can help them with motivation is to stop nagging, yelling, pushing, cajoling, or taking over—all of which will lead to resistance. Sometimes you get short-term compliance, but it's almost always followed by long-term failure. So, simply put, you cannot motivate. But you can inspire, encourage, and influence.

> *"Always do your best. What you plant now, you will harvest later."* OG MANDINO

To encourage motivation, there must be consequences to her decisions. If a girl doesn't go to bed early enough, she will experience the natural consequence of being tired (and most likely moody). After a full day of being tired and grumpy, which she'll notice and others will notice too, she may just be motivated enough to decide to go to bed earlier that night. You can gently point out to her and sympathize about how lousy the consequences feel. But if you just tell her to go to bed earlier, she will stay up late simply to spite you!

Find out what does motivate your girl. Ask questions like "What do you really want?" and "What are your goals and dreams?" Ask her these questions to explore what *could* motivate her, and work together on the answers. And sometimes, connecting what a girl really wants with what she needs to do to get there may just be the answer you need.

Notice what *does* work to motivate her. You might say, "I noticed that yesterday you did your homework right after school, but today you're waiting until later—what is the difference?" Try to understand her decision-making process. Put on a scientist's hat and investigate your daughter's choices, without judgment. Be curious and wonder. Your questions will prompt her to be

READ MORE
How to Motivate Your Kids,
by J.D. Nichol

self-reflective and help her understand herself and what motivates her. She can be a problem solver and make her own decisions.

When it comes to being motivated, we can't do it for them, but we can help them to learn to be motivated on their own and in their own ways. There will be much less conflict when we learn to talk to girls and figure out who they are and where their priorities and interests lie.

If you feel at a loss when it comes to motivating her, if you can't seem to get her to do anything, don't worry. You are not alone. When you get to this place, and maybe even feel like you want to give up, don't. When you see she is unmotivated, take this as an opportunity, even a sign, that she may not need you to motivate her—this will come from her—but that she does need you to connect with her. Lack of motivation may just be an entry point for better bonding, empathy, and understanding, and a time for reconnection.

CULTIVATING CONNECTION

Let's talk about:
- Motivation and what it means—the desire to get moving.
- What motivates her.
- How her motivation might increase—with learning and improving. Encourage her to trust that as she tries, she will become more motivated because she'll see the progress she is making toward her goals.
- The difference between intrinsic motivation (the rewards being a feeling of confidence, mastery of a skill, and achievement of a goal, for example) and extrinsic motivation (the rewards being grades, money, compliments, and praise, for example).

Let's try:

- Noticing when she does show motivation. What is working? For example, she may be motivated to complete her homework if she knows that when she's done, she is going to visit her friend. The next time she doesn't feel like doing her homework, ask her to think of what she can look forward to once her homework is complete.

- Encouraging a wide range of interests and activities, and providing her with as many opportunities as possible; variety may just motivate her and prevent boredom.

- Being an inspiring person or finding examples of young women who have been motivated to act, such as Taylor Swift or Jessica Alba.

- Dividing an uninteresting task into smaller parts, and finding ways to make it fun and interesting. For example, working in ten-minute intervals and taking dancing breaks. Or setting up some healthy competition: the first person to work for fifteen minutes straight gets to choose what break time looks like. Focus on what she can do. A little success, such as completing one task, will encourage her to keep trying.

- Teaching her to soak up success by basking in the glow of her accomplishments, even little ones, such as completing a task on her to-do list.

Ten Ways to Connect Starting Now

Connecting doesn't have to be complicated, and overthinking is not necessary. Here are ten simple ways to connect with a girl.

1. Give her a hug.
2. Look into her eyes and smile.
3. Tell her you are proud of her.
4. Say "I love you."
5. Go do something fun together.
6. Leave her a surprise note.
7. Begin a conversation with "Do you know what I appreciate most about you?"
8. Say yes to something she wants to try.
9. Notice when she takes a risk and shows bravery.
10. Start a dance party with just the two of you.

Going for Growth   27

FROM A VERY early age, girls are put into categories—easy baby or fussy baby, girly girl or tomboy—and as girls grow, they continue the categorization, putting themselves into limiting boxes—pretty or plain, good reader or poor reader, artist or mathematician, athletic or uncoordinated. Sometimes categorizing is a just a habit; other times it is an excuse so the girl doesn't have to try—she may be afraid of falling and failing, or of the pressure that comes with success. Whichever it is, this categorical thinking limits girls' development and places a ceiling on their progress. What is needed, instead, is a growth mindset.

Growth mindset is the belief that growing and learning is an ongoing, consistent process. If your intelligence can be developed with persistence, effort, and a focus on learning, it means you're never done. There's no destination you're always in progress.[1] This means intelligence can be cultivated and learned. This is in contrast to the concept of a fixed mindset, which holds that a person has a predetermined amount of intelligence, skills, and talents.

Stanford University professor of psychology Dr. Carol S. Dweck has conducted extensive research on fixed and growth mindset theory and has contributed to a major shift in thinking about student learning and intelligence. Dweck asserts that intelligence is a malleable quality that can be developed. Learners with a growth mindset believe they can learn just about anything. When a girl's attitude is positive, she is more likely to achieve positive results. And when we expect the best from her, she learns to do the same.[2]

Girls who embrace a growth mindset embrace the idea that growth is something they choose, and that their efforts contribute to the growth. This puts girls in the driver's seat, empowering them to take responsibility for their desired outcomes. Instead of giving up and saying, "I'm just not a writer," girls with a growth mindset say, "I'm going to work hard at writing every day to become a better writer."

> *"All who have accomplished great things have had a great aim, have fixed their gaze on a goal which was high, one which sometimes seemed impossible."* ORISON SWETT MARDEN

Supporting the idea of girls' growth mindset, Mary Cay Ricci, author of *Mindsets in the Classroom*, suggests that effort far exceeds intelligence and natural abilities in leading to growth and success.[3] Ricci explains the many benefits of a growth mindset, including greater risk taking, greater confidence and self-esteem, improved motivation, perseverance when things get tough and we're tempted to give up, an understanding of the connection between effort and success, feelings of empowerment, better performance, and increased likelihood of embracing challenges and truly enjoying the process of learning.

When girls learn to focus on the idea of growth as a process that takes both effort and time, and when they can let go of any categorical thinking in terms of their capabilities, they can fully embrace a growth mindset. Setting goals effectively in order to bring about desired outcomes is an important strategy for those with a growth mindset.

Goal Setting

There's no stronger tool in a strong girl's kit than goal setting. Goals help girls stay focused and excited about having something to work toward and to look forward to—and about their future. Girls who set goals come to understand that they are responsible for their own growth and success, and with practice they feel they can do anything they set their minds to, one small step at a time, thereby strengthening their growth mindset.

Goal setting encompasses choice and decision making about a desired goal, designing what the sub-goals and targets will look like, and executing the plan to achieve the goal. To set herself up for success, a girl ought to set goals that are sincere and specific; they should remind themselves of the goals as they work toward them, and protect them from being waylaid by obstacles. A successful goal-setter celebrates when she achieves her goal.

When it comes to goal setting, girls learn through experience—that they can reach their goals if they stop *talking* about what they hope to do and start *acting*, no matter how big or scary the goals seem. They understand that setting goals is the easy part, but that what matters most is their *attitude*—an "I know I can do this" approach—and the *effort* they are committed to putting forth. We need to remind them that setting and reaching goals can be difficult because it requires them to imagine the unimaginable, and risk requires bravery. So let's encourage girls to push themselves a little further, and champion them along the way, so that they never give up on the idea that everything can be achieved through persistence and practice.

To start, let's make sure their goals are what they *really, really, really* want to achieve. Girls often limit their thinking about goals to safe, easily obtainable goals. Encourage them to challenge themselves with goals that, at first glance, seem out of reach. She may have never considered continuing with higher education. Put it on her radar by asking her to imagine what the post-secondary experience would be like. Give her choices and help her hear what a goal could sound like. But let *her* choose, and let her experiment with changes. If she wants the goal she sets for herself, she'll be much more likely to work for it and persevere. Imagine if your boss set all your professional goals for you and you didn't have a say!

She may take time to explore the possibilities, so be patient, and be willing to explore with her. Be involved in the process, as she may need to watch inspiring videos or read books about other girls who have done great things. During this process, guide her to be realistic—matching the goal with her skill set, interests, and natural abilities and competencies. For example, if she is a runner, a realistic goal may be to set sixty minutes for completing a ten-kilometre race. If she likes musical theatre, a realistic goal might be trying out for a part in an upcoming musical. The key is to stretch her enough so she learns to reach for a new challenge while staying true to her skills and abilities.

Once she has chosen a goal, encourage her to get specific; the more specific the goal is, the more real it becomes. For example, she may set a goal to "Get better at school." Ask her what she means by this, and fine-tune the goal to something along the lines of "Get better at reading comprehension by reading and summarizing what I read for thirty minutes each day."

Write down the goal on a piece of paper or a poster board. There is a lot of power in the visual display of a goal—it will serve as a reminder to help her stay motivated. Encourage her to have some fun by decorating the page on which the goal is written. Then, work backwards with her to divide the goal into steps. These steps might include choosing a book that matches her reading level, and planning a time to commit to reading and gathering supplies (notebook, felt-tips, highlighters). Little steps help to get her started and create momentum. Small rewards along the way help as well—keeping her on task, motivated, and appreciative of her own efforts. Rewards might include a day off from chores or a new piece of equipment related to the task.

Be sure to predict and plan for obstacles—anything that could get in her way or derail her. It's realistic to expect obstacles. For example, she simply may lose interest in reading. If this is planned for ("When I lose interest, I will…"), she will know what to do. She may need a reminder at this point of all the times she has encountered obstacles, and how she overcame them. (See Chapter 20 to review how to turn setbacks into comebacks). Remind her of how she coped in the past and showed resiliency, and that she has what it takes to face difficulty head-on and work her way through with strength and boldness.

"The passion for stretching yourself and sticking to it, even (or especially) when it's not going well, is the hallmark of the growth mindset. This is the mindset that allows people to thrive during some of the most challenging times in their lives." DR. CAROL S. DWECK

Then all that's left is to get started and put in the time. Marking progress can be a great motivator. When she can see her own growth and just how far she's come, whether it's by using stars on a star chart or colouring in a bar graph or check marks, she will encourage herself to continue pushing toward her goal. Realizing she can do something she thought she couldn't do will be a powerful experience.

When she achieves her goal, recognize her effort and the journey. Celebrate in any way she wants, and help her give herself credit for her accomplishments. This is a great way to build up her competence. Use this time to evaluate how the process went—would she in retrospect do anything differently? Is there room for improvement? If part of the goal wasn't achieved, review why not—was it too vague or too challenging? Ask for her ideas for improvement. Then, when she's ready, help her set new goals. There's nothing more empowering than building on recent successes—this is going for growth!

CULTIVATING CONNECTION

Let's talk about:
- The definition of growth mindset and its advantages.
- The difference between a growth mindset and a fixed mindset.
- Goal setting and why it's important.
- How good it feels to accomplish something she wants to accomplish.
- Goals she has set for herself, and what helped her reach them.
- Goals she has set for herself, and what got in the way of reaching them.

Let's try:
- Focusing on effort rather than outcome: remind her that continued hard work, along with focus, will reap many benefits and personal bests; discourage comparisons to others; and always praise effort over outcome.
- Instilling self-belief—the belief that success is possible, and that she does have skills, and can also ask for help to develop her skill set. She needs to know that if she believes she will succeed, she will.

- Encouraging positive self-talk—encouraging phrases such as "I will succeed," which will help her along the way. Positive self-talk is the difference maker in thinking, choices, and behaviours.
- Asking her "If you could be anything or do anything, what would it be?" Ask her this question frequently as she learns to dream bigger and bigger.
- Giving her feedback; this is how she will learn best. Ask her how she wants feedback delivered, and work together on specific and timely feedback.
- Encouraging her to learn from her mistakes and practise "trial and error" learning.
- Helping her notice the specifics of her growth. Ask her to look back over how far she has come, so she can be reminded of her growth and motivated to continue to put forth the effort to grow. Charting progress improves awareness of growth and can be a fantastic motivator.
- Acknowledging often her effort and hard work (more than her results), and remembering to celebrate successes along the way.
- Taking one goal she wants to achieve, such as "I want to get better at horseback riding." Write down this goal on the top right-hand side of a piece of paper. Starting at the bottom left-hand side of the paper, write out the steps she may need to reach her goal, such as spending more time at the stables, asking her instructor for more feedback, questions she may need to ask in order to improve her horseback riding, research on horseback riding, and watching instructional videos on YouTube. List the steps in an order that works for her. Also consider obstacles that could get in her way and strategies for managing these obstacles. For example,

READ MORE
Mindset: The New Psychology of Success, by Dr. Carol S. Dweck

Mindsets in the Classroom, by Mary Cay Ricci

VIEW MORE
"Grit: The Power of Passion and Perseverance," TED Talk by Angela Lee Duckworth

"Not enough time" may be an obstacle. A strategy might be looking at her weekly schedule and prioritizing her horseback riding.

- Considering setting goals in many areas of her life: school, friends, home, and activities.
- Encouraging her to set new goals. Goals can help girls stay motivated and build on their successes; they also curtail boredom and stagnation.

Surviving to Thriving   28

I SEE AN amazing transformation begin to happen with the girls I work with when they decide to work on their own growth. They transition from merely surviving, to striving, to thriving.

I believe that this is the absolute highlight of my journey with emerging strong girls—to observe the pivot from "I feel like I can barely breathe, I'm so stressed out" to "I had a fight with a friend, and I am going to try talking to her to explain how I'm feeling" to "I studied for my humanities test and I thought I was going to fail, but I got my best grade ever!"

I have to smile when I see a new sparkle in their eyes, the revitalization of a once dull face—a sullen face that showed fatigue, discouragement, and surrender having evolved into priceless radiance and confidence.

At first, a girl really is just surviving. Consider any day in her shoes: it is packed with uncertainty about what to say and do, reprimands to herself for making the wrong choices, and a lot of stress and pressure to maintain her reputation and her cool amid chaos, confusion, and dramatics. As she tries to stay true to herself, she is pushed and pulled in every direction. She survives by focusing on one step at a time and just staying afloat.

Yet, as a girl grows, and as she begins to tap into her inner connection and inner power, she also starts to strive. Small risks become greater risks. Mistakes that once debilitated her become opportunities to learn and to become better, stronger. And where she perhaps used to become so easily unravelled, tangled, and derailed, she begins to learn that she now has the tools and strategies at her side and, no matter what, she can be there for herself.

As she becomes stronger and more confident—as we all wish for her—she'll come to the place of "What now?" She'll feel connected to her true self, full of love, self-compassion, confidence, and a sense of self-worth. She'll be comfortable in healthy relationships with a circle of friends, and have the ability to set solid boundaries—letting go of whoever or whatever is not honouring her authentic self. She'll be able to take ownership of her learning, embracing lifelong learning strategies and habits, and considering the difference she will make in the world. When she has deepened her connections to herself, others, and the world, then what? Well, then it's time to thrive!

"My mission in life is not merely to survive, but to thrive; and to do so with some passion, some compassion, some humour, and some style." MAYA ANGELOU

For a girl to thrive and become stronger each and every day, she'll need to realize and release the fear that is holding her back. Acceptance is the key. And she'll need to consider letting go of any thought, person, or circumstance that is holding her back from being her absolute best self. This can be hard—who wants to let go? But hanging on will only leave her feeling stuck. Safe, yes. But also stagnant. A little nudge from us, a little push out of familiarity and comfort, and just watch what she can do and all she can be!

When she considers the world she can step into—a world of possibility and potential, she can be inspired. With a clear vision of who she wants to be, with intention and the willingness to work, with the exuberant "I can do anything" feeling and a whole lot of courage, she can strive for excellence and become more authentic, whole, and connected. Thriving is the natural extension of surviving and striving!

Being part of this change will never cease to leave me feeling awestruck and inspired. Join me as we nurture, support, and grow strong girls.

READ MORE
Courage to Soar: A Body in Motion, a Life in Balance, by Simone Biles with Michelle Burford

CULTIVATING CONNECTION

Let's talk about:

- How she is surviving and staying afloat.
- How she can begin to strive: ideas she can try, risks she can take, baby steps that can move her out her comfort zone.
- All the possibilities she can consider in order to thrive— what does she *really, really, really* want for herself?

Let's try:

- Exploring her potential purpose by brainstorming what she wants to do and what matters most to her. Getting started on realizing these ideas can help her understand how she can thrive.
- Brainstorming all the possibilities when she considers the idea that "the sky's the limit." Together, write down all her ideas, and don't discount anything she says.
- Creating a vision board. On a poster board, glue pictures cut from magazines or downloaded from the Internet. Pictures can help her "see" what she wants in life. These pictures can represent both material things, such as a home she wants to live in or a car she wants to drive one day, and things that represent inner happiness, such as a heart for love (of herself and others) and a beach to symbolize peacefulness.

Conclusion

THERE IS A lot of talk about girls' experience and the challenges they face day to day. It's my intention to shift us from *talking* about girlhood, and what's going sideways with girls, to actually *doing* something about supporting girls as they make their way forward. I know there are challenges and numerous concerns with growing strong and healthy girls. And I am deeply convinced that anything is possible when we invest our attention, intention, connection, and action.

Growing strong girls may have sounded like an impossible task, but you accepted the challenge. I am so proud of you. It is my hope that you feel differently now: more empowered and equipped than ever with the knowledge and tools you need.

And what girls need most of all—though some days, this may be hard to believe—is you. Trust me on this one: girls need us. They need our empathetic listening, they need our ideas and advice, they need our life experience and wisdom, and they need our time and presence. Girls also need our guidance, our care, our compassion, and, ultimately, our love. Sometimes just being there is *more than enough*. Trust me on this one as well.

Let's meet girls where they are, and commit to journeying alongside them as they go, and to challenging them to be their best, strongest, most authentic selves.

Be bold and brave as you embrace the ideas you've come up with by working through this book. Have the courage to change—one small act at a time. Trust yourself—that you have what it takes, and you know what to do. Decide to take an active role in a young girl's life because she needs you and because you can.

We can do this, together. We got this! And remember this one last thing: you are not alone. It takes a village. I am so very thankful for the village I always dreamed of being part of, the village I am proud to be included in today as I continue my work with girls and young women, and the expanded village I envision the ideas in this book will create. You are now part of that village! Let's work together to grow strong girls—an ambitious goal, but one worth reaching.

Acknowledgements

Girls

First and foremost, I have to thank all the girls in my life; they have been an essential and integral part of my journey and inspired the ideas in *Growing Strong Girls*. It is a privilege to know you, to nurture your growth, and to be your champion in any way I can. Thank you for inviting me into your inner world and sharing with me—your concerns, your struggles, your pain, and your hopes and dreams. You have taught me so much about how to be stronger.

Parents

To all the parents I have journeyed alongside, I truly appreciate how you have entrusted your most precious gifts to me, your daughters. You have inspired me each and every day with your unwavering care, love, and devotion to raising happy and healthy girls. Honestly, I do not know how you do it, but I am so thankful that you do. I relish all your kind words of encouragement, especially on days when I felt I was no longer making a difference. Your emails, phone calls, and candid conversations with me have really affirmed and encouraged me to stay the course.

LifeTree Media

The only reason this book has come to fruition is because of the amazing team at LifeTree Media. Since my first email proposing what seemed to be a preposterous idea and vision, I have received nothing but genuine care, interest, and support. I know it is because of the cornerstones of LifeTree Media, the values-driven desire to publish books that help, heal, and inspire, that I have loved every step of my publishing journey and have learned that anything is possible with the right combination of talented people. Dreams really do come true if you continue to search for the "magic" of a team who believes in you, supports you, and challenges you to produce your very best work.

To my publisher, Maggie Langrick, thank you for believing in my idea to turn my passion for my work with girls into something real and tangible. You are the fighter and champion I needed, and you came into my life at the perfect time. To my editor, Michelle MacAleese, who I liked from our first conversation, simply because of your fantastic sense of humour. You told me there was no reason we couldn't have fun as we collaborated, and you were right. You not only made the entire creating process fun, but you held my hand tightly, as I asked you to do. To Paris Spence-Lang, marketer by day and writer by night, I cannot believe how much you made me laugh. Your youthful sprit is infectious and, in stressful times, you were exactly what I needed. My gratitude to Setareh Ashrafologhalai, my designer; thank you for listening and hearing me. Thank you to Judy Phillips, Avril McMeekin, and Zoe Grams for all your valuable insights.

The Wishing Star

To everyone at The Wishing Star, my safe place and my second home. I am so proud to be part of the amazing work you all do, and I love the clear vision you hold, looking at the world through the eyes of a child. What an inspiring team of authentic practitioners, who understand big and little people alike and the importance of relationship and authentic connection. Vanessa, you know I adore you. From our first early morning coffee and chocolate meeting, I felt how much you cared, and I was lifted up by your exuberance and belief in my work with young girls. You nurtured me through my challenges, you always make time for me, and guess what? I survived, just as you said I would.

Friends and Family

I sincerely thank you all for listening to me as I grew into my own strength and confidence, personally and professionally. I appreciate all the insights you provided, all the nurturing and love you gave me, and all the lessons you taught me. Thank you for being my mirrors to reflect back to me what you saw in me, when I wavered in believing in my own potential. I know you gave me your best ideas and a great deal of your time. I am indebted to you all; you have been my greatest teachers of forgiveness, happiness, and love.

Kelvin

You have taught me and shown me what it really means to be strong. This book would not exist if it weren't for your clarity and articulation about inner strength, inner power, and the importance of being who you are. You have opened my eyes to a world I was afraid to look at—the truth. And it is because of you I have felt empowered to take big risks, to work hard and push myself every day, and to be the very best version of myself that I can be. I am so thankful I met you and so happy that our "chance encounter" became something real. It is a privilege to journey alongside you in this life.

Resources

RESOURCE 1. The Self-Worth Manifesto and Ways to Help Her Feel Strong

CREATE A LIST of statements that can serve as her guidelines for what she wants and how she can honour her self-worth. Here are some examples to get you started.

- I have the right to say no.
- I have the right to be respected by others.
- I have the right to choose nurturing and positive relationships.
- I have the right to say I don't agree and to give my opinion.
- I have the right to feel and express all my feelings.
- I have the right to be proud of my accomplishments.
- I have the right to recognize my needs and to ask for what I need.
- I have the right to change my mind.
- I have the right to walk away from teasing or mean people.
- I have the right to be treated with love and kindness.
- I have the right to make mistakes.
- I have the right to take risks.
- I have the right to cancel plans.
- I have the right to be silent and to not talk when I don't feel comfortable.

RESOURCE 2. Positive Power Statements

THESE POSITIVE STATEMENTS are meant to help your girl get started in identifying who she is, what she will do, and what she can do to be stronger. Ask her to choose one (or more) from each category that best describes her in the moment. You may want to write these out on cue cards and then post them on her bulletin board as reminders. The right power mantra can instantly build her up anytime she needs it!

"I Am" Statements

- I am confident.
- I am strong.
- I am bold.
- I am inspired.
- I am growing.
- I am learning.
- I am powerful.
- I am brave.
- I am flexible.
- I am healthy.
- I am happy.

- I am kind.
- I am beautiful.
- I am authentic.
- I am expressive.
- I am helpful.
- I am self-aware.
- I am supported.
- I am talented.
- I am balanced.
- I am capable.

"I Will" Statements

- I will learn the way I need to learn.
- I will always try my best.
- I will never give up.
- I will always be there for myself.
- I will take positive risks.

- I will ask for help when I need help.
- I will always be true to myself.
- I will let go of unhealthy thoughts.
- I will take time to be self-aware.

"I Can" Statements

- I can do anything.
- I can set boundaries.
- I can trust myself.
- I can express all my feelings.
- I can take all the time I need.
- I can show myself self-compassion.
- I can stand up for myself and others.
- I can ask for what I need.
- I can mean what I say and say what I mean.
- I can learn whatever I want to learn.
- I can pass the test.
- I can make a choice.

RESOURCE 3. Common Connection Concerns

COMMON CONCERNS	IDEAS FOR GROWTH
Expecting too much from others and from life.	Teaching her to lower her expectations of others (not of herself and not her own standards).
Trying out many personalities and identities.	Encouraging her to explore and be who she really is, to be true to herself.
Experiencing bully behaviour.	Teaching her to share and express any feelings of shame or embarrassment; practising standing up to bullies and getting help immediately.
Making social comparisons.	Helping a girl develop a clear sense of self and focus on personal best.
Excluding/forming social alliances against one another.	Encouraging connection and inclusivity.
Talking about her problems to everyone else except the person with whom she has the problem.	Teaching direct communication and privacy.
Having "all about me" thinking.	Reminding her of perspective, and to take a step back and understand that some things have nothing to do with her.
Making assumptions and employing A-to-Z thinking (when she takes leaps in her thinking).	Challenging her assumptions and helping her break down her thoughts into smaller, more manageable ones.

COMMON CONCERNS	IDEAS FOR GROWTH
Trying too hard.	Teaching her to trust that things will work out, and to relax into life and situations.
Holding unhealthy attachments.	Helping her make good choices in friends. Ask her "Is this person healthy for you or unhealthy?" and "Do you feel better or worse when spending time with this person?"
Catastrophizing or exaggerating social errors.	Teaching her that there is no such thing as a social error; teaching her to accept, learn, let go, and move on (and the sooner, the better).
Misinterpreting social cues.	Exploring alternative interpretations of social situations (for example, what else it can mean when someone doesn't say "Hi" back to her).
Having tunnel vision.	Helping her use radiant thinking to explore all options, solutions, and possibilities.
Compromising her values and voice in order to fit in socially.	Encouraging her to be clear on her boundaries and on what she thinks and feels.
Blaming others and life in general for her problems.	Teaching responsibility and ownership; she can't help the cards she was dealt, but she has choice about how to manage her problems.
Judging and criticizing other girls.	Redirecting her focus on her strengths and positive traits.
Having the "disease to please."	Helping her practise self-care and taking care of her needs first, before helping others (she cannot give what she does not have); teaching boundaries—over-helping is stepping over her own boundaries.
Worrying too much about what others think.	Guiding her to set her own goals and embrace her uniqueness, while teaching her to worry less.
"Connecting" through screens and websites.	Encouraging her to make real connections and not derive her self-worth from social media and "Likes."
Being mean and needing power over other girls.	Helping her stand up to meanness (and never giving in, by being strong, certain, and secure in herself; reminding her to always surround herself with positive people for extra support.
Being easily influenced by other girls, even when their values are different.	Worrying less about fitting in; focusing on being real and authentic.

RESOURCE 4. Top Tips for Homework and Studying

HOMEWORK AND STUDYING can be stressful activities for everyone. Here are my top tips to support girls when it's time to hit the books.

1. Create a clear and clean work surface and a distraction-free desktop (disabling pop-ups and alerts).
2. Promote brain health with water, nutritious food, and sleep.
3. Help her set a homework goal for her time doing homework (a to-do list to work through), which teaches time management and organization.
4. Encourage her to be creative and use several learning styles at once. Have fun trying mnemonic devices (linking information to pictures, rhymes, or phrases) and incorporating drawing and pictures, mind maps, and quizzes.
5. Ensure she reads and understands all instructions and directions.
6. Guide her to practice the "step-by-step learning method" by identifying the steps required and doing one step at a time. Breaking it down is especially helpful for more difficult tasks that may overwhelm her.
7. Practise daily review (of what she learned) and preview (looking ahead at what she will be learning).
8. Help her manage stress with deep breathing, visualization techniques, positive thoughts, and imagining success.
9. Practise spaced studying: fifteen to twenty minutes at a time, with short breaks (no screens on break time).
10. Guide her to review her textbook by skimming, scanning, previewing, and asking questions—the more familiar she is with her books, the more effective her study time can be.

NOTE If helping her with homework and studying becomes too stressful or frustrating for either of you, or there are too many tears, seek outside support.

RESOURCE 5. Empowerment Songs

MUSIC IS ONE of the greatest tools we have to reconnect to our inner selves, rejuvenate from the inside out, and put a smile on our faces. If you need a playlist for some of the activities I share in *Growing Strong Girls*, or want to make an uplifting and inspiring mix for your own day, check out some of these songs (listed here in no particular order). And visit www.LindsaySealey.com, where I share about my new favourite artists and songs.

- Brave—Sara Bareilles
- Up We Go—Lights
- Happy—Pharrell Williams
- Superwoman—Alicia Keys
- Firework—Katy Perry
- Stronger Together—Katy Perry
- Rise—Katy Perry
- Roar—Katy Perry
- Just Like Fire—P!nk
- Let It Go—James Bay
- Shake It Off—Taylor Swift
- A Woman's Worth—Alicia Keys
- Stronger (What Doesn't Kill You)—Kelly Clarkson
- Wouldn't It Be Nice—The Beach Boys
- Stand by Me—B.B. King
- (Your Love Keeps Lifting Me) Higher and Higher—Jackie Wilson
- Ain't No Mountain High Enough—Marvin Gaye and Tammi Terrell
- My Boy Lollipop—Millie Small
- My Girl—The Temptations
- Signed, Sealed, Delivered (I'm Yours)—Stevie Wonder
- I Will Survive—Gloria Gaynor

- Respect—
  Aretha Franklin
- Man! I Feel Like
  a Woman!—
  Shania Twain
- No More Drama—
  Mary J. Blige
- When You Believe—
  Whitney Houston and
  Mariah Carey
- I Didn't Know My
  Own Strength—
  Whitney Houston

- Stupid Girls—P!nk
- Because You Loved
  Me—Céline Dion
- The Power of Love—
  Céline Dion
- Let It Go—
  Idina Menzel
- Don't Worry,
  Be Happy—
  Bobby McFerrin
- Lovely Day—
  Bill Withers

NOTE These songs and music videos are suggestions for girls to listen to and have been chosen for their upbeat rhythm and empowering lyrics, but in selecting these songs, I am not necessarily presenting the individual artists in all aspects of their personal lives as ideal role models for girls.

RESOURCE 6. Positive Role Models

IT CAN BE hard to find positive and healthy role models for a girl these days, and who she decides to follow is going to be who inspires her the most and who she feels most connected to. By creating a list of positive role models to follow and learn from, she is more likely to make positive and healthy choices herself.

Consider these powerful girls and women:

- Simone Biles
- Nitika Chopra
- Chelsea Clinton
- Lena Dunham
- Bethany Hamilton

- Mindy Kaling
- Haley Kilpatrick
- Jennifer Lawrence
- Amy Poehler
- Malia Obama

- Sasha Obama
- Meghan Trainor
- Carrie Underwood

- Emma Watson
- Malala Yousafzai

NOTE These suggestions of people for girls to follow have been selected because of their positive attributes, such as grit, determination, confidence, strength, and achievement. It's important that you choose the role models best suited for your girl, with the understanding that role models can't possibly be perfect, nor should this be the expectation.

RESOURCE 7. Body Wisdom

THE INFORMATION OUR bodies provide to us is an invaluable tool available to us all. By paying attention to her body, a girl can slow down and listen to her inner voice, improve her health and state of mind, and feel a sense of wholeness and interconnectedness to all that is around her.

Begin with the Breath

Breathing deeply is simple but can have a big impact. Instead of getting diverted by rapid-fire thoughts and the never-ending hum of background anxiety, a girl can use mindful breathing exercises to calm down. They will affect the digestive, respiratory, circulatory, and nervous systems, grounding her body in an awareness of its sensations, and making it possible for her to regulate emotions and guide attention inward.

To begin, encourage her to take four seconds to take a deep breath in through her nose, four seconds to hold her breath, and four seconds to breathe out through her mouth. One suggestion here is to ask her to imagine she is breathing in positive feelings of love, confidence, and courage, and breathing out negative feelings of fear, worry, and frustration. Breathe in and breathe out, just like that. Ideally, the two of you can do this breathing exercise together.

Once she gets the hang of it, she can try attaching her breath to an intentional thought. Invite her to do a "positive reframe" of a less-than-positive thought: instead of "I have so much to do and not enough time," she can recite "I have more than enough time." The pairing of breath with a simple mantra can be transformative!

Body Scan

Once she is feeling more calm, invite her to use do a body scan. For this technique, ask her to find a comfortable position, sitting or standing, and close her eyes. Then direct her to breathe slowly and steadily and move her attention throughout her body, from her head to her feet, pausing at tight, stuck, or sore areas. The goal is to relax each part of the body as she is paying attention to it, and to become an observer of her body, with a healthy distance for perspective, without judgment. When she encounters a tight place, she can breathe into it—literally breathing in while holding her attention on, say, a clenched jaw or a knot in her stomach. When she breathes out, she will feel a difference, however small. Once she has scanned her entire body, she can rest for one to three additional minutes, breathing normally, then gently open her eyes.

To wrap up, invite her to quickly check in with herself and then tell you how she is feeling or was feeling during the body scan. Encourage her to get curious about where in her body she feels various feelings and to notice if, for instance, she feels anger in her jaw, fear in her shoulders, or joy in her heart. Ask her to take note so that next time she notices a feeling, she can be even more attuned to these signs in her body.

Through breathing and awareness exercises like these, the brain marries inner and outer experiences, increases inner calm, and rejuvenates cells and energy. And on a practical level, she will learn how to pay attention when "something's wrong" or she feels "weird."

Movement Is Medicine

Another effective way for girls to connect with their bodies and that sense of wholeness and interconnectedness is through physical activity, whether vigorous or gentle, and as is possible and enjoyable for her body. Some girls may find movement makes it much easier to feel inwardly connected, as opposed to sitting still. (Some girls may find even the few minutes it takes to perform a body scan excruciating, if trauma or intense feelings are coming up. If you are concerned about a girl's mental health or physical welfare, contact a professional.)

Not every girl will enjoy the same physical activities. Some girls will love dancing, swimming, or skateboarding; others, horseback riding, martial arts, or ringette. Some will enjoy team sports, others will love taking long walks with the dog. Remember, whatever she loves to do is the best fit for her.

When the families I work with are looking for a healthy movement practice, I recommend yoga, for many reasons: it's easy to start up, it's generally available and affordable (especially at community centres), and its benefits to focus, flexibility, and energy are endless, for every body at any age. This ancient practice, which originated more than five thousand years ago in India, is about bringing mind, body, and spirit into unity to promote health, peacefulness, and harmony.

The benefits of yoga are more than physical. Yoga gives girls a way to balance out their moods, enhance their fitness, improve their sleep, and develop a healthier body image. Yoga can help a girl to open up—both physically and on other levels, as she considers the idea of growth, stepping out of her comfort zone, and expanding her sense of self. A little "push" with a challenging pose can encourage her to feel she can do it. If she can do it in yoga, why not in life?

Positive Body Language

Another powerful tool to access one's body wisdom is confident body language. What a girl says with her body says a lot about her. Confident body language looks like this: standing tall with shoulders back, holding the head high and making eye contact, with feet planted firmly and arms by the sides. Consider what this posture declares to the world, compared with a body that slouches, shoulders sagging, the torso closed off, and chin tucked in.

The awesome thing is that shifting into a confident posture will show others that she is prepared to engage confidently. And with more positive energy and by experiencing positive interactions, she will feel more confident. Over time, confident body language can lead to a positive frame of mind—so fake it 'til you make it!

These simple practices—deep breathing, body scanning, physical activity, yoga, and positive body language—will go a long way to training a girl's brain and body (because they are really one and the same) to support her in growing strong in focus, concentration, and self-awareness. Remember, paying attention to the body and learning from it will look different for each unique girl and will change over time; it's all about choosing whichever activities feel best for her and supporting her in becoming more energized and more empowered. You'll know it's right when she feels less stress and more joy.

Notes

Introduction

1. Sue Johnson, "Hold Me Tight," *Psychology Today* January 1, 2009, https://www.psychologytoday.com/articles/200901/hold-me-tight.

2. L. Alan Sroufe, Elizabeth A. Carlson, Alissa K. Levy, and Byron Egeland, "Implications of Attachment Theory for Developmental Psychology," *Development and Psychopathology* 11 (1999): 1–13.

3. Amir Levine and Rachel S.F. Heller, *Attached: The New Science of Adult Attachment and How It Can Help You Find—and Keep—Love* (New York: Penguin, 2011), 21–22.

CHAPTER 1 Who I Am

1. Sarah Kay, "If I Should Have a Daughter," TED Talk, March 2011, video, https://www.youtube.com/watch?v=0snNB1yS3IE&t=24s.

CHAPTER 3 Perfectly Imperfect

1. Brené Brown, *The Gifts of Imperfection: Let Go of Who You Think You're Supposed to Be and Embrace Who You Are* (Center City, MN: Hazelden, 2010), 56.

2. Kristin Neff, *Self-Compassion: The Proven Power of Being Kind to Yourself* (New York: HarperCollins, 2011), 8.

CHAPTER 4 Self-Care and the Whole Girl

1. Michael Pollan, *In Defense of Food: An Eater's Manifesto* (New York: Gale, 2008), 9.

2. Patricia Adler and Peter Adler, *The Tender Cut: Inside the Hidden World of Self-Injury* (New York: NYU Press, 2011), 2.

3. Isaiah 30:15, New International Version, Biblica, https://www .biblegateway.com/passage/?search=Isaiah%2030:15&version=NIV.

CHAPTER 5   Girl in the Mirror

1. Julia V. Taylor, *The Body Image Workbook for Teens: Activities to Help Girls Develop a Healthy Body Image in an Image-Obsessed World* (Oakland, CA: Instant Help Books, 2015), 23.

2. Media Smarts, "How Marketers Target Kids," http://mediasmarts .ca/digital-media-literacy/media-issues/marketing-consumerism/ how-marketers-target-kids.

CHAPTER 6   Mind Full to Mindful

1. Tanya Basu, "Why More Girls—and Women—Than Ever Are Now Being Diagnosed with ADHD," *New York,* January 20, 2016, http:// nymag.com/scienceofus/2016/01/why-more-girls-are-being- diagnosed-with-adhd.html.

2. Goldie Hawn, *10 Mindful Minutes: Giving Our Children—and Ourselves— the Social and Emotional Skills to Reduce Stress and Anxiety for Healthier, Happy Lives* (New York: Penguin, 2011), xxvi.

3. Derek Thompson, "If Multitasking Is Impossible, Why Are Some People So Good at It?" *The Atlantic,* November 17, 2011, http://www .theatlantic.com/business/archive/2011/11/if-multitasking-is- impossible-why-are-some-people-so-good-at-it/248648/.

4. Lisa Quast, "Want to Be More Productive? Stop Multi-Tasking," *Forbes,* February 6, 2017, https://www.forbes.com/sites/lisaquast/ 2017/02/06/want-to-be-more-productive-stop-multi-tasking/ #11833b6255a6.

5. Kim D. Rempel, "Mindfulness for Children and Youth: A Review of the Literature with an Argument for School-Based Implementation," *Canadian Journal of Counselling and Psychotherapy* 46, no. 3 (2012): 201–20.

CHAPTER 7 Life Balance

1. Shimi Kang, *The Dolphin Way: A Parent's Guide to Raising Healthy, Happy and Motivated Kids, without Turning into a Tiger* (Toronto: Penguin, 2014), 252.

CHAPTER 9 Gratitude

1. Lucie Hemmen, *Parenting a Teen Girl: A Crash Course on Conflict, Communication & Connection with Your Teenage Daughter* (Oakland: New Harbinger Publications, 2012), 166.

2. Sara Abdulla, "A Serious Article about Laughter," *Nature*, December 17, 1998, http://www.nature.com/news/1998/981217/full/news981217-2.html.

CHAPTER 10 Exploring Spirituality

1. Amish Shah, "Kids and Happiness: Can Children Really Experience Spirituality?" Project:Yourself, n.d. [2014?], http://projectyourself.com/blog/kids-and-happiness/.

2. Ken Shigematsu, *God in My Everything* (Grand Rapids, MI: Zondervan, 2013), 20.

CHAPTER 12 Words Matter

1. Trisha Prabhu, "Rethink before You Type," TEDxTeen, October 2014, video, https://www.youtube.com/watch?v=YkzwHuf6C2U.

CHAPTER 13 Express Yourself

1. Louann Brizendine, *The Female Brain* (New York: Harmony Books, 2006), 31.

2. Lisa Damour, *Untangled: Guiding Teenage Girls through the Seven Transitions into Adulthood* (New York: Ballantine, 2016), 86.

3. Leslie Greenberg, "Emotion and Cognition in Psychotherapy: The Transforming Power of Affect," *Canadian Psychology* 49, no. 1 (2008): 49–59.

4. Brené Brown, "The Power of Vulnerability," TED Talk, June 2010, video, https://www.ted.com/talks/brene_brown_on_vulnerability.

CHAPTER 15 Girls Can Be Mean

1. Rachel Simmons, *Odd Girl Out: The Hidden Culture of Aggression in Girls* (New York: Mariner Books, 2011), 3.

CHAPTER 18 Social Media and Keeping It Real

1. Aric Sigman, "The Impact of Screen Media on Children: A Eurovision for Parliament," in *Improving the Quality of Childhood in Europe,* edited by C. Clouder, B. Heys, M. Matthes, and P. Sullivan, 88–121 (Brussels: European Council for Steiner Waldorf Education, 2012), https://pdfs.semanticscholar.org/e1b2/97f00e4e6bca0a0d85cdd-5b9924e487444ea.pdf?_ga=1.258096713.291919705.1488669032.

CHAPTER 19 Screen Time and the Tangled Web

1. Heather Loney, "Canada's Youth Are Highly Connected, Girls Face Different Rules Online: Study," Global News, January 22, 2014, http://globalnews.ca/news/1098160/canadas-youth-are-highly-connected-girls-face-different-rules-online-study/.

2. Jane Wakefield, "Children Spend Six Hours or More a Day on Screens," BBC News, March 27, 2015, http://www.bbc.com/news/technology-32067158.

3. Carolyn Meggitt and Tina Bruce, *CACHE Level 3 Early Years Educator for the Classroom-Based Learner* (London: Hodder Education, 2014).

4. Nicholas G. Carr, *The Shallows: What the Internet Is Doing to Our Brains* (London: W.W. Norton, 2011), 120.

CHAPTER 21 Loving Learning

1. Collaborative for Academic, Social, and Emotional Learning, "What Is Sel?" CASEL, http://www.casel.org/what-is-sel/.

2. Singapore, Ministry of Education, "Social and Emotional

Learning," n.d., https://www.moe.gov.sg/education/programmes/
social-and-emotional-learning.

3. Victor Gecas, "The Social Psychology of Self-Efficacy," *Annual
Review of Sociology* 15 (1989): 291–316.

4. Ferris Jabr, "The Reading Brain in the Digital Age: The Science
of Paper versus Screens," *Scientific American*, April 11, 2013, https:
//www.scientificamerican.com/article/reading-paper-screens/.

5. Helene M. Sisti, Arnold L. Glass, and Tracey J. Shors, "Neurogenesis
and the Spacing Effect: Learning over Time Enhances Memory
and the Survival of New Neurons," *Learning Memory* 14, no. 5
(May 2007): 368–75, https://www.ncbi.nlm.nih.gov/pmc/articles/
PMC1876761/.

CHAPTER 22   Learning for Life

1. Howard Gardner, *The Unschooled Mind: How Children Think and How
Schools Should Teach*, 2nd ed. (New York: Basic Books, 2011).

2. Mind Tools, "VAK Learning Styles," https://www.mindtools.com/
pages/article/vak-learning-styles.htm.

3. Daniel J. Siegel and Tina Payne Bryson, *The Whole-Brain Child: 12
Revolutionary Strategies to Nurture Your Child's Developing Mind, Survive
Everyday Parenting Struggles, and Help Your Family Thrive* (New York:
Bantam, 2012), 15–16, emphasis in original.

CHAPTER 24   What's Ahead? Planning and Preparing for the Future

1. Maria Menounos, *The EveryGirl's Guide to Life* (New York:
HarperCollins, 2011), 5.

CHAPTER 25   Who's in Charge? Choices and Decision Making

1. Diane Dreher, "Do Today's Women Have Too Many Choices?"
Psychology Today, February 6, 2012, https://www.psychologytoday.
com/blog/your-personal-renaissance/201202/do-todays-women-have-
too-many-choices.

CHAPTER 27 Going for Growth

1. Mary Cay Ricci, *Mindsets in the Classroom: Building a Culture of Success and Student Achievement in School* (Waco, TX: Pruffock Press, 2013), 3.

2. Carol S. Dweck, *Mindset: The New Psychology of Success* (New York: Ballantine Books, 2016).

3. Ricci, *Mindsets in the Classroom*, 3.

Permissions

GRATEFUL ACKNOWLEDGEMENT is made to the following sources
for permission to reprint from previously published material.

Quotation on p. 27 from *Self-Compassion: The Proven Power of Being
Kind to Yourself* by Kristin Neff, Ph.D. Copyright © 2011 by
Kristin Neff. Courtesy of HarperCollins Publishers.

Quotation on p. 35 from *The Curse of the Good Girl: Raising Authentic
Girls with Courage and Confidence* by Rachel Simmons, published
by Penguin. Used by permission.

Quotation on p. 57 from *The Dolphin Way: A Parent's Guide to Raising
Healthy, Happy and Motivated Kids, Without Turning into a Tiger*
by Shimi Kang, published by Penguin. Used by permission.

Quotation on p. 68 from *The Path to Love* by Deepak Chopra,
published by Harmony Books. Used by permission

Quotation on p. 114 from *Odd Girl Out: The Hidden Culture of
Aggression in Girls* by Rachel Simmons. Copyright © 2002 by
Rachel Simmons. Reprinted by permission of Houghton Mifflin
Harcourt Publishing Company. All rights reserved.

Quotation on p. 137 from *The Shallows: What the Internet Is Doing to Our
Brains* by Nicholas Carr, published by W. W. Norton & Company.

Quotation on p. 164 from *The Whole-Brain Child* by Dr. Daniel J. Siegel
and Dr. Tina Payne Bryson, published by Bantam.

Every effort has been made to contact the copyright holders; in the
event of an inadvertent omission or error, please notify the publisher.

About the Author

LINDSAY SEALEY holds a master's degree in Educational Leadership from San Diego State University. A passionate girl advocate, she has worked in education, consulting, curriculum development, and special education for over fifteen years and is the founder and CEO of Bold New Girls, a unique and comprehensive teaching and coaching company for girls and young women, and their parents, teachers, and caregivers. Lindsay lives in Vancouver, Canada.

You can visit Lindsay online at www.LindsaySealey.com. If you like what she has to say, you can leave her a review on Amazon, Goodreads, or your favourite online place to buy and find out about books.